THE NEW ECONOMY – THE PERFECT ECONOMY

God showed me the Future, train me and ask me to Solve the World's problems

OOGLE

PARTRIDGE

Copyright © 2019 by Oogle.

Library of Congress Control Number: 2019916556
ISBN: Softcover   978-1-5437-5496-4
         eBook   978-1-5437-5497-1

All rights reserved. No part of this book may be used or reproduced by any means, graphic, electronic, or mechanical, including photocopying, recording, taping or by any information storage retrieval system without the written permission of the author except in the case of brief quotations embodied in critical articles and reviews.

Because of the dynamic nature of the Internet, any web addresses or links contained in this book may have changed since publication and may no longer be valid. The views expressed in this work are solely those of the author and do not necessarily reflect the views of the publisher, and the publisher hereby disclaims any responsibility for them.

Print information available on the last page.

To order additional copies of this book, contact
Toll Free 800 101 2657 (Singapore)
Toll Free 1 800 81 7340 (Malaysia)
orders.singapore@partridgepublishing.com

www.partridgepublishing.com/singapore

ABOUT THE AUTHOR

A Licenced Real Estate Agent, Insurance Agent and Futures Trader.

I invented Intelligent OS which is part of Artificial Intelligence and 3D Search which is the tagging of images used in Facial Recognition and DeepFakes in 2012 and I did not patent it but licenced it under Creative Common Licence. which anyone can use it without royalties but must acknowledge my credits.

I am equipped with a brain that is 10000 times the normal and is even faster than the most advanced neural computer. God taught me everything and He command me to solve all the problems of the world. I can create an invention every hour and technologies out of this world. I can sample data and create hundreds of view to find any solution you want and know what the results is even without trying the full load. That is my secret of my extraordinary skills. All I need is the internet to watch a video, read a news report or any scientific report and identify the problem and insight. Within 1 hour I can get you any solutions and paths or strategies you need to succeed. My brain activity functions 5 times a normal person and my blood pressure is now 260, and the sugar in my blood is about 28 on average without any ill effects, without any complications. A normal person will end up having a stroke. A miracle? What does this means? I am capable of hacking, studying and researching into anything I want, calculate the probability and risks and use it for prediction, and use it for finding any solutions I want, and by studying everything I already know the outcomes of anything I want, so I already know what will succeed without wasting resources.

I was discharged from bankruptcy in 2016 but I have managed to achieve a semi-retired lifestyle thru a strict system of financial goals which I will explain to you. I have helped my ex-wife achieve financial freedom by getting insurance which she has received almost S$1,000,000 in payouts so I do not have to worry about supporting her and my children. During my divorce I gave my half share of my house to her and told her to rent out our HDB flat for regular payments of $2,500 to feed my children so I have the freedom not to worry about my family finances. Nobody has helped me even though my aunt is a millionaire and my mom has a rental HDB which she derive rental income for her retirement, I never take a single cent from them. My brother has a doctorate and he is a lecturer in Nanyang Polytechnic but we could not get along because of her wife which is very money faced. My mom has invested more than S$50,000 for my brother to study in Australia and with his own inheritance of S$65,000, he totally spent all on his overseas education. I will depend on my own skillset of IT trainnng and the use of Internet and Social media to raise funds for the poor and help non profit organisation. Even though I have yet to achieve all my financial goals but along the way I know I will achieve them, it is only a matter of time. I am straight in line for my inheritence of a 4 rm HDB flat which my mother owns and when the right time come I will have enough monies to do what I want to do. Even though because of my bankruptcy which was recently discharged nobody believes I could do it but I have a system and knowledge how to achieve great amounts of monies, which I will only review when I achieve financial success. So now bear with me as I await all my financial goals and if you are able to help, donate some money thru paypal on my website so I am able to use it to help the poor and non profit organisation.

I do not believe living in a life of luxury and even when I achieve financial success, I will still stay in my 1 room rental flat and spent less than S$1k a month on food. I do not need a lot of monies to sustain myself even though Singapore is such an expensive place to stay. My retirement plans is to accumulate at least S$1 million so I don't have to worry about money when I grow old.

I am writing a book to detail all my hardship and the sacrifice I made until I achieve financial success so that others can follow on the path I has created. There is NO SHORTCUT TO SUCCESS and if you are looking for a shortcut this book is not for you. There is no guarantee in The New Economy with a Degree in Education you will find success and I have chosen a method to write everything down so that you can gain all the necessary knowledge by taking certificates in various disciplines instead and learn how to money manage you way to success.

I am not a saint, and I am not here to start another religion, I am a normal human being who has desires like anyone else and sin like everyone else, but enlightened that anything in this world like Money, Fame, Power, and Material things does not matter to me, as I follow my Lord's ways, and I have reached a state that I have discovered all the secrets that man longed for, and I am truly blessed by God. They have priests who can perform miracles like rising people from the dead to healing and casting the devils out, but my only power will be total control of the weather and stopping disasters like typoon and hurricane after I achieved God's work. I already is able to handle a Global Financial crisis, Famines or Epidermic and will use all my knowledge to prevent wars and conflicts which will cause sufferings to everyone.

Since 2005 when I started my works, nobody believed me and nobody helped me. My kickstarter campaign only raise $2 and was a failure, all my websites did not contribute a single cent. Instead everything I do was interfered and I was not even able to raise money hu borrowings from Singapore and US lenders. What is the real issue when all my projects I do benefits mankind? Today with God's help I have waited for the right time when all will fall in to place.

Facebook : GilbertTanTS

Patreon : GilbertTanTS

https:\\www.geniussolutionssg.com

https:\\www.itfornonprofitsg.org

MY VISION OF A "PERFECT" MARKET AND ECONOMY

Demand can be determined before Supply, where the use of Price will determine your global market share, everything can be traded in the "New Economy" with exchanges that facilitate trading in goods and services, and the future can be determined at a future price from the present, debts can be bought and sold, like bonds with a recurring interest like dividends, where money is used to solve the world's problems, healthcare, ageing, jobs and welfare are just factors of demand and supply, where the correct pricing mixed with a set of priorities will lower it to a sustainable level, every governments need to learn the tricks and tweaks, by studying all the best models from the world, if digital money is put in the right perspective, priorities and goals are more important, a world where there is no inflation or deflation, the access of funding with austerity measures, will help the creation of wealth with a multiplier, steady inflation will indirectly promote growth, being poor will not be a deterent, you must be able to plan and execute, all components require the endorsement of all, the co-operation of all, to build a better future, with the participation of the UN, IMF and World Bank, a world without nuclear weapons. The "New Economy" is the Age of Information, where every markets is tracked with 24 hours data to facilitate trading of goods and services 365 days a year, prosperity is for everyone, jobs for everyone, where you do not worry about putting food on the table, technology advances will benefit mankind, high growth is not an issue, if you get things right now.

When everyone realised I have the solutions to solve the Global crisis by creating Demand and GDP growth in a sustainable manner by setting priorities and goals with reforms and changes, will you seriously support the "New Economy" and Free Trade and the United Nations run by Jesus?

The rise of the barter trade exchanges. The futures exchanges trade not only in commodities, but contracts of good and services to be delivered in the future, with easy financing and terms of default clearly spelled out, even instruments of debts can be easy traded.

This vision can be realised within a lifetime ie less than 50 years to totally eradicate poverty from the face of this earth, trading is done every second of the day, when you need money, it can be realised almost immediately, free trade will be expanded a thousand times over, so what is high GDP growth not achieveable, a future of a "perfect" market?

FOUNDATIONS OF THE NEW ECONOMY

Lessons need to be learned, the capacity of markets, to maximise demand and not to overproduce. If you know you are overproducing, and still attempts too, you will see your rewards dwindle. My beliefs is that there is a market for everyone, to maximise your profits, to cancel destructive competition, by finding new products and services, which is part of the "new economy". Knowledge is the key, to maximise your returns.

Let me give you an example. In the MP3 war, you have Apple leading the market, followed closely by Creative. Let's assume there are only two markets, the US and Singapore. And the local demand for Singapore is 10,000 units per month and 90,000 units for export, the US market is 100,000 units and a furthur 150,000 units for export. Production capacity for Apple is 100,000 units per month and Creative is 25,000 units. The life cycle for each product is about 9 months whereby after that, price will decrease at a rate of 20% per quarter until the lowest price of 20% whereby the product will be handed over to OEM manufacturers. Directors, manufacturers, and stragedy planners, what do you have in mind to maximise your profits? What stragedy will you use? How do you acquire business intelligence? Do you let your product be determined by market forces? What happens when you overproduce? How do you increase your branding? How do you create brand loyalty?

Let's make this scenerio as real as possible.

If you can sell Creative MP3 in Singapore at S$500 per unit but only S$400 in the US market, and the market share in Singapore is 40/60 and in the US is 20/80 for Creative/Apple. What are your options?

And if you are able to control these factors, what will you chose?

1) Increase capacity to produce by another 15,000 units (Creative) at an investment of $100K to streamline your production lines.
2) Spent $100K at publicity campaign to increase sales in local market by 10% and US market at 8%.
3) Let's say, all factors are under your control. How do you create branding and loyalty?

Anyone can provide me the answers? I will post them at this website. The idea is to find all the paths and options to maximise profit and create branding or loyalty. Everyone needs to harvest an intimate knowledge of whatever market you are in to maneuver against the market and competition. When I see a demand, I will race at maximum capacity, and when I see a falling market, I will pack up and reinvent.

With in depth analysis, I have provided you the questions to find out the answers, to find out the different paths you can take, to maximise profits at minimum risk, to see the entire view of the market.

And if I am even crazy, I will merge all this information, with accounting and budgeting info, seeking all the paths with the limitation of a budget, can I accurately assess my risks? Best of all, if I expand my vision, to include all the world's market, including forex exchange, do you get dizzy all of a sudden? No, not really, everything can be segmented, with very clear objectives, goals and relationships, that is something, nobody has tried to do.

PRINCIPLES OF THE "NEW ECONOMY"

The "New Economy" is based on, preventing destructive competition. I believe there is a market for everyone, and competition is fine, but when competition start eroding profits until a loss, it is destructive competition. Everyone should help your neighbours. And if by helping you I created a friend rather than an enemy, I have created my future when I meet you headlong in direct competition, you will definitely give way to me. And if I teach you how to solve your own problems, you will be eternally greatfull, creating less an enemy rather than an ally, which will help you surged ahead. Economic schools need to reteach the young, how to read economic data and useful information, how to identify markets and determine demand and supply, and if a market is satuated to move away from it, find new markets or create new goods and services, to reinvent oneself. There is a lifespan in every good and service, and when it is no longer economically viable, it's time to move on, to reinvent yourself, to find new markets or goods or services. Imagine, if you do not follow what I have taught you, even if you find success yourself and fell all your enemies, no one could afford to buy your goods and services when all are poor and cannot afford the riches you have created. FTAs, economic reforms, economic liberalisation, and economic co-operation are all part of the "New Economy". When you have goals, to reach a developed country's status like the Swiss, "thoughts of wars", the lessons of history, will have no place in the "New Economy". If any country tries to do otherwise, sanctions will be imposed, trade restrictions, total blockade by the rest of the partners. Then poverty will be a lesson learned. The fundamentals of the "New Economy", is that every human being is created equal, you do not need another superior race, to control another, learn how to solve your own problems, by adhering to strict principles, "you will reap what you sow", being lazy has no place, being stupid is because you do not want to learn.

By embracing the "New Economy", in less than a lifetime, poverty will entirely be eraticated, from the face of this earth, poverty will only be, the domains of the warlike, on those who will rather use violence and their fists, to solve a problem. The message is very clear, "If you invest in destruction, you are only going to destroy your own self, if you invest in economic reforms, you are going to save yourself from poverty." Likewise, example "if you got an Aid's problem, and you are not going to invest sufficient resources, do you think the problem will go away?". Most developing countries, have a major problem, of raising healthcare costs for the elderly, the maintainance and payout of pension funds, but little do they realise, the benefits of preventive medication, they only solve problems when it is too late, too costly. The promotion of a healthy lifestyle, the investment to promote health, and making sure your citizens are economically viable, even having enough resources, by planning for old age, is saving you future money, rather than being a drain to your coffers. There are jobs for everyone, even in old age, it's just that productivity is not as high, and if you have invested in improving your knowledge when young, you will be a valuable tool, its just the access to old age funds will help you continue, a more comfortable productivity, a more comfortable lifestyle. Fact is, you don't need to wipe tables in a foodcourt or collect cans and garbage if you plan for it, invest in knowledge and health, have sufficient savings to maintain a proper job and lifestyle. In the future, I see a developed Financial market that will utilise risk-based components to built a wide range of financial products, where the contribution of CPF ordinary can be use with co-insurance, to add on to the retirement fund, to ensure a more higher returns, to lock up savings for retirement. The Medisave can also be utilised, to buy other products, to minimise risk upon sickness, for outpatient care, or with other products to reinsure the cash component. A lot will depends on financial institutions, the pooling of resources, the reinvention of financial products with risk components, to cater to the needs of the market, and the ultimate goals of the government.

I believe once the demands are established, there will be an automatic participation both by the private and government, to solve this teething problem encountered by all the nations.

THE NEW ECONOMY – A BRIEF OUTLOOK

Preventing Destructive Competition

Most important Rule : "Never allow your customers to compare apple to apple, you will create destructive competition and will erode your profits until you cannot survive."

You need to identify what is "Horizontal competition" and "Vertical Competition".

Horizontal competition is having a common product like ice cream but based on different brands, different pricing, and different flavors to separate yourself from the competition.

Vertical competition is destructive competition where the customer cannot identify your product from your competitor's causing you to lose control which will result in loss of pricing.

The highest ROI can be achieved from determining Demand before Supply, where with today's high rent and manpower costs, nobody wants to use the traditional methods of manufacture of producing an oversupply and causing a loss of price, not maximising resources.

Fishing in the New Economy

The New Economy is a Knowledge Based Economy, where survival means you need the knowledge of the markets, a lifelong learning experience for education and never stop trying to achieve success.

It does not matter if you need to follow the traditional path of getting a University Degree, what matters is you learn a skill to make a living, and be equiped with the knowledge of markets to ensure your survival.

Never go in blindly without doing a bit of research, find out the costs of acquiring the skill, the potential of it's marketshare or earning potential, that is the basic skills of an entrepreuner.

Always find out from the competition and it pays to diffentiate your products or services within a radius of about 2 km, the consumer will always buy from the lowest cost unless it is a service you provide.

First mover advantage. Normally those who start a trade early will have an advantage based on location, never go head to head with destructive competition, you will always lose in the end.

In business profit is always the basic motivation factor and if you can sell less to earn more, why will a manufacturer favour another who have to sell even higher quantity to earn the same profits you earn.

It is always connections or Kuan Si that will get you favourable terms with your expertise. If not why would someone will give you business and let you earn money? Unless of course you got a lot of money.

Gone are the days where only profits or money is the only motivating factor, there are social causes as well. Others maybe the connections it brings, without a knowledge of the markets, you can forget about Fishing in the New Economy.

Information on local demographics, lifestyle and Incomes are the Big Data of the New Economy. You can get great insights by looking at financial data or statistics or sampling, it will give you great advantage over identifying trends before the full impact is felt by others.

Determining Demand Before Supply

Nobody use the traditional methods of manufacture which will cause an oversupply and a drop in price.

Every manufacturer will now determine Demand first by taking orders based on a selling price which would have factored in his costs before Supplying the goods at a predetermined future date.

Therefore Demand will meet Supply to meet the highest ROI possible. Characteristics will be smaller orders at a more frequency but profits will not be eroded.

This helps the Global Economy as profits are guaranteed and many people will be willing to invest. Indirectly it will also create jobs for many people and there will be increments in salary when more profits are re-invested.

Knowing Market Dynamics

The entire global economy is like musical chairs, each country sitting on a chair with a role until it upgrades itself to another seat.

Understanding Macro and Micro Economics, can you tell the difference between domestic markets and overseas markets?

How interbank interest rates affect currency markets and the cost of money?

Hot money inflows will always goes to the most transparent economies which gives the highest ROI.

Domestic and Foreign markets, it is still Location, Location and Location

That is why you must be very familiar with the local demographics, the population, their lifestyle and their habits so as to identify the Demand and Supply of any goods or services.

It will teach you why within a certain walking distance of eg 2km if you start another shop selling the same goods and services, chances is you will not make any decent profits unless you are able to create horizontal competition.

Can you differentiate the same hairdressing services? An Indian shop charging $8 per haircut, a Fashion saloon charging $16, a Haircut chain charging $10 and another charging $3.90? What will happen to this location when correction occurs?

The Framework of Problem Solving

A person can only buy 2 homes in his lifetime, 1 to stay, another to rent out. Beyond that, he will have to pay increased capital gain tax. Rich people who can buy numerous homes should put them in a Holding company, and enjoy Tax consessions.

There should be a compulsary contribution from your salary to your retirement fund like CPF, which can be utilised for housing and healthcare.

Affordable healthcare can be achieved with insurance, and the separation of the business of providing advice and the dispensing of medication to get the lowest cost possible.

Insurance is a business of pooling of resources to solve a need. Money collected is pooled, excess monies are reinvested to get higher returns, where mortality rates and statistics determine the claims, so even expensive healthcare can be even covered if the public participates.

Retail Banking should be separated from Investment Banking based on Risk Taking to ensure stability of the Banking System where deposits are guaranteed but not risk taking.

The New Economy is a Knowledge Economy and everyone should be taught the pathway to success.

A lifelong learning experience is necessary which means you do not necessary have to get a University Education to succeed, and in your lifetime you may change your job but do not have to worry about finding a new job.

There should be Social Enterprise and Non Profit to give a helping hand on retraining and those who falls through the cracks, and the government's responsbilty to contribute towards it.

As every country is a member of the United Nations, there will be funds from World Bank/IMF especially on Social engineering and Non Profit where every dollar contributed by governments will be matched without repayment based on needs.

But first every country needs to first endorse it and every country needs to have equal rights to have their voices heard, the end of wars and weapons of mass destruction, then peace and prosperity will prevail.

The Creation of Digital Money (Bitcoin)

Money have to be backed by Gold, or it will become Banana money, and massive inflation will cause it to lose it's value very quickly because of loss of confidence.

QE is a temporary fix for the domestic economy as it depegs the value of the currency to Gold, causing a devaluation of the currency due to the printing of money.

The effect will be the a drop in currency value which will translate to cheaper exports but more expensive imports. It should not be used as a permanent fix as long term it will affect the debts market and your bond yield will start dropping in price until nobody wants to buy your debts.

The mechanics of Present and Future money. Inflation will help fuel asset appreciation and over the long term, money will depreciate in value but assets will appreciate.

Due to wages not able to keep up with inflation, your future earnings to buy assets will be greatly reduced. Something needs to be done to address this issue for the salaried worker. Our children needs a future where their purchase of their homes need to be calibrated for affordability according to their future income.

Based on inflation of 2% yearly your home will increase in price by 200% in a hundred years but the increase is more acute. Do you think your children's salary will increase by the same amount? Sadly No.

Everybody needs Oil now for energy and do you think Oil will last forever? At about US$100 per barrel will it raise to US$500 in fifty years time? Nobody can then afford it for cars anymore but aircrafts. By then we will develop Nuclear Fusion energy.

Money is used as a Tool to efficiently allocate resources. Do we need physical money in future? No. We can create Virtual money. Sometime in the future when we reached a Perfect Economy we can even have Virtual money, then No money at all when we do not need to allocate resources anymore with God as our supplier of all our needs.

Before you start clamouring to buy your house now consider this fact: Can you afford to pay your mortgage with your future earnings? What have you done to protect your future earnings?

You need to create the Climate and the Environment for Investments. If everyone in the Global economy perceives that there will not be a recovery or growth will we have future investments?

In a New Initiative without the Federal Reserve printing money, there will not be inflation or hyper-inflation, there will not be a depression or a recession, because the New World uses Digital money backed by God's Technologies so we can use as much as we want without Governments suffering the ill effects of over printing money. The entire world will be run by the United Nations with Jesus controlling it.

So there is no Shortcut to Success. We need to solve all the problems of the Old Economy, institude reforms and bring confidence back again.

Live within your means. Never overspend.

In order to achieve Financial Success in future, you got to live within your means and never overspend. You need to have a percentage of your Income which you can save monthly to invest in yourself to get passive income. If you are living from paycheck to paycheck you are locked in the poverty cycle and can never improve your lifestyle

THE PROBLEM WITH AN IMPERFECT MARKET

Concept Theory 1
"Money will flow into the most free market offering the maximum returns."

Concept Theory 2
"How to maximise Capitalism? Where Demand=Supply will give you the maximum returns."

Concept Theory 3
"The New Economy is a Perfect Market, where the old economy is an imperfect market. Markets will react immediately with the free flow of information to correct any flaws in demand and supply."

Concept Theory 4
"Globalisation is the co-operation of every markets, every governments."

Concept Theory 5
"By solving Capitalism, and the use of money, resources will be maximised for maximum gain."

Concept Theory 6
"With the Internet, information flows freely and the markets reacts immediately."

Concept Theory 7
"Investments is engaging the markets all the time, hedging against your risks, for returns."

Concept Theory 8
"In either a Bull or Bear market, money is still made, all of the time."

Concept Theory 9
"Small money can be used to hedge against a future event requiring a Large Sum with the use of complex derivatives, underwriting the risks/returns ratio and the pooling of resources."

"As such, the flow of hot money is very disruptive to the fragal economy and causes all kinds of problems like hyper-inflation and imbalances, and rises of prices in commodities and assets. But liquidity of money in capitalism is essential for growth in the economy, how do we strike a balance? By keeping interest rates low for a prolong period will not encourage savings but spending, but how long of your future earnings can you afford to borrow against?

Liberal controlled re-expansion of credit (Refinancing and recapitalisation) is a better answer for liquidity in the markets than pure liquidity in the hands of a few with the credit ratings. Everything from houses, cars, businesses, commodities, assets can qualify for refinancing and reassessment of value/risks for the portion that has already been paid up(100%) with the borrower's credit ratings in consideration. Unsecured loans can be extended to up to 6 times his monthly salary instead of the present 3 times. It will indirectly spur consumption and more investments into the future by the expansion of credit for economic growth, ensuring the soundness of financial institutions with confidence in the future. It will also redistribute wealth evenly for the haves and haves not. Since the risks of a global asset bubble has been corrected and taken away, it is back to the basics of fundamental growth."

THE CO-RELATION BETWEEN DEMAND AND SUPPLY, INFLATION AND INTEREST RATES

Under the Old Economy, Asset inflation and Interest Rates will always create a Bubble, and the FED cannot control the Economy by just printing money, it is just kicking the can down the road. In the New Economy, Bitcoin as a digital currency has no inflation, and the demand and supply of bitcoin is tightly regulated, central bankers cannot anyhow create credit in the banking system which will cause a bubble, you are in control of your own money, so all the risks are taken away from the economy, there will not be a financial collapse. Contributed by Oogle.

What is Inflation?

Inflation is the rate at which the general level of prices for goods and services is rising and, consequently, the purchasing power of currency is falling. Inflation is a key concept of **Macroeconomics.** Central banks attempt to limit inflation and avoid deflation in order to keep the economy running smoothly.

Relationship of Interest Rate and Inflation

Inflation and interest rates are often mentioned in the same breath, and this is because **Inflation** and interest rates are closely related. In the United States, baseline interest rates are set by the central bank, the Federal Reserve Bank also known as the Fed. The Fed meets eight times a year to set short-term interest rate targets. During these meetings, the CPI and PPIs are significant factors in the Fed's decision, because the Fed, as well as other major central banks, has a specific interest rate target in mind for the economy to achieve, usually 2-3% annually.

In order to control high inflation, the central bank increases the interest rate.

When interest rate rises, cost of borrowing rises. This makes borrowing expensive.

Hence borrowing will decline and as such the money supply(i.e the amount of money in circulation) will fall. A fall in the money supply will lead to people having lesser money to spend on goods and services. Hence, they will buy a lesser amount of goods and services. This, in turn, will lead to a fall in the demand for goods and services.

With the supply remaining constant and the demand for goods and services declining; the price of goods and services will fall

In low inflationary situations; the interest rate is reduced. A fall in interest rates will make borrowing cheaper. Hence, borrowing will increase and the money supply will also increase. With a rise in money supply, people will have more money to spend on goods and services. So; the demand for goods and services will increase and with supply remaining constant this leads to a rise in the price level i.e inflation.

Inflation and **interest rates** are often linked and frequently referenced in **macroeconomics**. Inflation refers to the rate at which prices for goods and services rise. In the United States, the interest rate, or the amount charged by lender to a borrower, is based on the **federal funds rate** that is determined by the **Federal Reserve** (sometimes called "the Fed").

In general, as interest rates are reduced, more people are able to borrow more money. The result is that consumers have more money to spend, causing the economy to grow and inflation to increase. The opposite holds true for **rising interest rates**. As interest rates are increased, consumers tend to save as returns from savings are higher. With less **disposable income** being spent as a result of the increase in the interest rate, the economy slows and inflation decreases.

Under a system of **fractional-reserve** banking, interest rates and inflation tend to be inversely correlated. This relationship forms one of the central tenets of contemporary monetary policy: central banks manipulate short-term interest rates to affect the rate of inflation in the economy.

To understand how this relationship works, it's important to understand the banking system, the **quantity theory of money** and the role interest rates play.

Fractional-Reserve Banking

The world currently uses a fractional-reserve banking system. When someone deposits $100 into the bank, they maintain a claim on that $100. The bank, however, can lend out those dollars based on the **reserve ratio** set by the central bank. If the reserve ratio is 10%, the bank can lend out the other 90%, which is $90 in this case. A 10% fraction of the money stays in the bank vaults.

As long as the subsequent $90 loan is outstanding, there are two claims totaling $190 in the economy. In other words, the supply of money has increased from $100 to $190. This is a simple demonstration of how banking grows the money supply.

Quantity Theory of Money

In economics, the quantity theory of money states that the **supply and demand** for money determines inflation. If the money supply grows, prices tend to rise, because each individual piece of paper becomes less valuable.

Interest Rates, Savings, Loans and Inflation

The interest rate acts as a price for holding or loaning money. Banks pay an interest rate on savings in order to attract depositors. Banks also receive an interest rate for money that is loaned from their deposits.

When interest rates are low, individuals and businesses tend to demand more loans. Each bank loan increases the money supply in a fractional reserve banking system. According to the quantity theory of money, a growing money supply increases inflation. Thus, a low interest rate tends to result in more inflation. High interest rates tend to lower inflation.

This is a very simplified version of the relationship, but it highlights why interest rates and inflation tend to be inversely correlated.

The Federal Open Market Committee

The **Federal Open Market Committee** (FOMC) meets eight times each year to review economic and financial conditions and decide on **monetary policy**. Monetary policy refers to the actions taken that affect the availability and cost of money and credit. At these meetings, short-term interest rate targets are determined. Using **economic indicators** such as the **Consumer Price Index** (CPI) and the **Producer Price Indexes** (PPI), the Fed will establish interest rate targets intended to keep the economy in balance. By moving interest rate targets up or down, the Fed attempts to achieve target employment rates, stable prices, and stable **economic growth**. The Fed will raise interest rates to reduce inflation and decrease rates to spur economic growth.

Investors and traders keep a close eye on the FOMC rate decisions. After each of the eight FOMC meetings, an announcement is made regarding the Fed's decision to increase, decrease or maintain key interest rates. Certain markets may move in advance of the **anticipated interest** rate changes and in response to the actual announcements. For example, the **U.S. dollar** typically **rallies** in response to an interest rate increase, while the **bond market** falls in reaction to rate hikes.

ECONOMICS REQUIRES "A REVOLUTION IN TECHNIQUE"

Would economists be better off starting from somewhere else? Some think so. They draw inspiration from neglected prophets, like Minsky, who recognised that the "real" economy was inseparable from the financial. Such prophets were neglected not for what they said, but for the way they said it. Today's economists tend to be open-minded about content, but doctrinaire about form. They are more wedded to their techniques than to their theories. They will believe something when they can model it.

Mr Colander, therefore, thinks economics requires a revolution in technique. Instead of solving models "by hand", using economists' powers of deduction, he proposes simulating economies on the computer. In this line of research, the economist specifies simple rules of thumb by which agents interact with each other, and then lets the computer go to work, grinding out repeated simulations to reveal what kind of unforeseen patterns might emerge. If he is right, then macroeconomists, like zombie banks, must write off many of their past intellectual investments before they can make progress again.

Mr Krugman, by contrast, thinks reform is more likely to come from within. Keynes, he observes, was a "consummate insider", who understood the theory he was demolishing precisely because he was once convinced by it. In the meantime, he says, macroeconomists should turn to patient empirical spadework, documenting crises past and present, in the hope that a fresh theory might later make sense of it all.

WITHOUT DESTRUCTIVE COMPETITION, YOU GET "REAL MARKET PRICES"

With "Real Market prices", you get higher wages
If Destructive competition will erode profits
Getting "Real Market prices" will ensure you get maximised profits
The "New Economy" is a knowledge based economy
Where you learn how to maximise profits
Without "Destructive competition"
Like musical chairs every country has a role to play
Every domestic economy
"Maximised profits = maximised returns"
In the end everyone get richer
This is the real "Asset Enhancement" scheme
"What goes around will come around"
Citizens get richer, pay higher taxes
Governments get richer to fund their supluses
To take care of those who fall thru the cracks
In a lifetime poverty and hunger will not exist anymore
We will then reach equilibrium "The Perfect Economy".

DETERMINING DEMAND BEFORE SUPPLY WITH TOTAL CONTROL OF SUPPLY CHAIN

by THE NEW YORK TIMES
12:53 PM Oct 24, 2011

Producing objects of desire without a price premium over competitors has proven a winning combination

NEW YORK – Something unexpected has happened at Apple, once known as the tech industry's high-price leader. Over the last several years it began beating rivals on price.

People who wanted the latest Apple smartphone, the iPhone 4S, were able to get one the day it went on sale if they were willing to wait in a line, spend at least US$199 (about S$250) and commit to a two-year wireless service contract with a carrier.

Or they could have skipped the lines and bought one of the latest iPhone rivals from an Apple competitor, as long as they were willing to dig deeper into their wallets. For US$300 and a two-year contract, gadget lovers in the United States could have picked up Motorola's Droid Bionic from Verizon Wireless, or they could bought the US$230 Samsung Galaxy S II and US$260 HTC Amaze 4G, both from T-Mobile, under the same terms.

Apple's new pricing strategy is a big change from the 1990s, when consumers regarded Apple as a producer of overpriced tech baubles, unable to compete effectively with its Macintosh family of computers against the far cheaper Windows PCs. But more recently, it began using its growing manufacturing scale and logistics prowess to deliver Apple products at far more aggressive prices, which in turn gave it more power to influence pricing industrywide.

Apple's innovations – including products like the iPhone, iPad and the ultrathin MacBook Air notebook – are justifiably credited for their role in the company's resurgence under its chief executive and co-founder Steve Jobs, who died on Oct 5.

But analysts and industry executives say Apple's pricing is an overlooked part of its ability to find a large audience for those products beyond hard-core Apple fans. Case in point, Apple sold more than 4 million iPhone 4S smartphone over its debut weekend.

People can still easily find less expensive alternatives, with less distinctive and refined designs, to most Apple products. Within the premium product categories where Apple is most at home though, comparable devices often do no better than match or slightly undercut Apple's prices.

"They're not cheap, but I don't think they're viewed as high-priced anymore," said Mr Stewart Alsop, a longtime venture capitalist in San Francisco.

Prices in the ultrathin notebook category are an illustration of Apple's strategy. While there are much cheaper laptops for sale, ranging all the way down to bargain-basement netbooks that cost a few hundred dollars, Apple's MacBook Air has become a hit among computer users seeking the thinnest and lightest notebooks available. The product starts at US$999 for a model with an 11-inch screen.

On Oct 11, the Taiwanese computer maker Asus introduced its answer to the MacBook Air, a sleek device with a brushed aluminum body that uses Windows. But it was unable to undercut Apple; the Asus computer also starts at US$999. Samsung's wafer-thin Series 9 notebook, with a comparable set of features, costs US$1,049.

The computer maker Acer, however, began undercutting the cheapest MacBook Air this month with an US$899 ultrathin notebook, the Aspire S series, that has a bigger screen.

The original MacBook Air catered to a more rarefied audience when it came out in early 2008, priced at a whopping US$1,799 for a model with a 13-inch screen. A year ago Apple revamped the notebook to make it thinner and smaller and reduced its entry-level prices to US$999 and US$1,299 for models with 11-inch and 13-inch screens.

Mr Jean-Louis Gassee, a venture capitalist and former Apple executive, said there was a "collective gasp" at how low Apple priced the new MacBook Air.

The aggressive pricing, analysts say, reflects Apple's ability to use its growing manufacturing scale to push down costs for the crucial parts that make up its devices. Apple has also shown a willingness to tap into its huge war chest – US$82 billion in cash and marketable securities last quarter – to take big gambles by locking up supplies of parts for years, as it did in 2005 when it struck a five-year, US$1.25-billion deal with manufacturers to secure flash memory chips for its iPods and other devices.

By buying up manufacturing capacity ahead of time, Apple forces its competitors to scramble for the parts that are still available, raising costs for their products, analysts say. Apple is the biggest buyer of flash memory chips in the world, according to the research firm iSuppli.

Mr Gassee said Apple's pricing decision on the MacBook Air made it clear that Apple's management of its supply chain had become a "strategic weapon".

Another example of that was Apple's decision to price the entry-level iPad at US$499 when it was introduced early last year, hundreds of dollars lower than many analysts expected.

"I think everyone was stunned at the cost of the iPad," said Professor John Gallaugher, who works on information systems at Boston College. "It was a very competitively priced device."

For a time, Apple's biggest competitors were unable to go below the iPad's price with their own tablets. When Motorola's Xoom tablet hit the market in February, the cheapest model available without a wireless service contract was US$800. Motorola later released an entry-level model with more storage than the least expensive iPad, priced at US$599.

After lacklustre sales, Apple's major competitors are now finally undercutting the iPad on price, though it is not clear how sustainable that approach is. Motorola recently announced a plan to offer an entry-level Xoom tablet for US$379 at Best Buy stores for a limited time. After Hewlett-Packard, having missed sales goals, announced plans to discontinue its TouchPad line of tablets, it dropped the price of its cheapest model to a fire-sale US$99.

The most credible challenge to the iPad is likely to come from Amazon's US$199 Kindle Fire tablet, which goes on sale next month. While analysts say they believe Amazon will lose money on each device sold, the Internet retailer's plan is to use the device to encourage purchases of other Amazon products and services, like e-books.

WHY INFINITE COMPETITION IN A DOMESTIC MARKET WILL ULTIMATELY CRASH THE MARKET

Competition between global players will spur competition
Create innovations and lower the cost of goods
But infinite competition will cause destructive competition
Lowering the price until your profit = zero
Then you have a collapse where no goods can be produced anymore
Especially in a domestic market
Horizontal competition is good as it will create
A broad spectrum of goods as diverse as the oceans
But Vertical competition will cause the same type of good
To drop drastically in price until profit = zero
So it is unsustainable and unproductive
So everyone must co-operative to prevent destructive competition
Where the knowledge of markets will cause
Everyone to shy away from goods and services
That has very low margins or profits
Ultimately get higher profits and wages
Welcome to the New Economy.

CONCENTRATE ON WHAT GIVES YOU THE GREATEST RETURNS FIRST

By Tom Polansek and Charles Abbott
WASHINGTON | Fri Mar 30, 2012 4:57pm EDT

(Reuters) – U.S. farmers will plant the most corn in 75 years to cash in on higher prices, topping expectations at the expense of soybean and spring wheat sowings, according to a U.S. government report on Friday.

The dramatic expansion raised hopes that the next harvest would ease razor-thin supplies that have kept corn prices near historic highs.

The Agriculture Department, in a separate report, said supplies in storage as of March 1 were smaller than expected, making a big crop imperative.

"Going forward, it's going to be all about the planting weather," said Don Roose, president of U.S. Commodities.

Despite the early prospects for a bumper crop, Corn, wheat and soybean **futures** rose strongly on the surprisingly tight grain stocks. Corn for delivery in May went "limit up," rising by the maximum amount allowed in a day of 40 cents. The climb of 6.6 percent to $6.44 a bushel was the biggest gain for corn since Oct 11.

Soybeans were up 3 percent, to a six-month high of $14.02 a bushel, and wheat was up nearly 8 percent, the biggest increase since Oct 11.

FARMERS GEAR UP FOR BIG YEAR

The farm sector is enjoying a boom that dates from 2006 as food demand rose worldwide and biofuels helped spur crop production. With farm income at record highs, farmers have updated their tillage equipment and built more storage bins, making business for equipment makers like Deere & Co and AGCO Corp, seed companies such as Monsanto Co, bin manufacturers such as Brock Grain Systems, owned by Berkshire Hathaway, and processors such as Archer-Daniels-Midland Co (ADM).

The increase in corn acres and decline in soy acres is particularly positive for fertilizer producer CF Industries, which is weighted more heavily in the production of nitrogen fertilizer need to grow corn, said Jeff Stafford, equity analyst for Morningstar. Soybeans don't require nitrogen fertilizer. CF Industries was up 2.2 percent at 185.5, while rival fertilizer maker Mosaic was up just 0.3 percent at 55.43. Bunge Ltd, the world's top oilseed processor, could take a hit from the decline in soy plantings, Stafford said. However, grain companies also could make more money by transporting increased volumes of crops around the world. "For a grain trader like Bunge, they make more money from the higher volumes of food that are shipped," he said. Bunge was up 1.7 percent at 68.38, while ADM was up 1.4 percent at 31.7. Deere was up 0.5 percent to 80.90.

MORE CORN IN THE TOP CORN STATE

Another year of full-throttle output is on the horizon. USDA estimates growers will plant the largest area to the eight major field crops — corn, wheat, rice, cotton, soybeans, sorghum, barley and oats — since 1998 and up 2 percent from 2011.

In USDA's annual prospective plantings survey, farmers said they would expand corn planting by 4 percent from 2011, which exceeded analyst expectations or 94.72 million acres. Iowa, the No 1 corn state, would plant a record amount of land to corn.

Soybean plantings were projected to fall 1 percent nationwide from last year to 73.9 million acres, increasing concerns about tightening global supplies of the oilseed due to poor harvests in South America. Analysts had expected soy plantings to increase to 75.393 million acres.

"Acreage is expected to shift to corn," the USDA said. In many states, corn offers higher returns than competing crops.

In Iowa, corn planting would be up by 4 percent while soybeans drop 6 percent. Nebraska, No 3 in corn, would expand corn area by 5 percent while trimming soybeans by 4 percent and wheat by 11 percent. Illinois, No 2 in corn and soybeans to Iowa, would boost soybean area by 100,000 acres, or 1 percent, while cutting corn by the same amount.

LARGEST CORN PLANTINGS SINCE 1937

Big corn plantings should replenish a stockpile that is forecast to shrink to its lowest level since 1996 by the Sept 1 end of this marketing year. If farmers stick to their plans, it would be the most corn planted 97.2 million acres in 1937.

USDA estimated farmers will plant 12 million acres of spring wheat other than durum, with a record low number of acres seeded in South Dakota. That is down 3 percent from last year and below the average trade estimate of 13.313 million acres.

USDA's projection for a total wheat planted area of 55.9 million acres was up 3 percent from 2011 but well below the average analyst estimate of 57.422 million acres.

Growers intended to plant 13.2 million acres of cotton, down 11 percent from last year, and 2.56 million acres of rice, down 5 percent, according to the USDA report.

With normal weather and yields, the corn harvest would be a record 14.5 billion bushels, up 10 percent from the mark set in 2009, according to Reuters calculations. Soybeans would total 3.2 billion bushels, the fourth largest on record. The wheat harvest would be 2.1 billion bushels and cotton growers would pick 18 million bales.

TIGHT SUPPLY

The U.S. corn stockpile was down 8 percent from a year ago, the government said, with consumption running faster than traders expected.

In a quarterly report, USDA said there were 6.009 billion bushels of corn in storage on March 1, 2 percent less than traders expected. Some 3.6 billion bushels were consumed during the quarter, equal to 30 percent of the 2011 crop.

Traders estimated consumption would be 4 percent smaller than USDA estimated.

Soybean stocks were estimated by USDA at 1.372 billion bushels, up 10 percent from a year ago but 1 percent smaller than traders expected.

Wheat stocks totaled 1.201 billion bushels, according to USDA, down 16 percent from a year ago and 2 percent less than traders expected.

(Editing By Russell Blinch and Alden Bentley)

Principles of the New Economy

Corn Highest Return
Soya bean Second Highest
Wheat Third Highest

By concentrating on fulfilling the highest pricing for corn, you get maximum returns, where the price of corn will lower until equilibium, for fulfilling the demand for corn, when price of corn lowers to producing the corp of corn = costs where profit = zero, it is time to move on to fulfill the next crop which is Soya bean, this will go on eternally, and the forces of demand and supply will ensure equilibrium, where is corn price = costs where profit = zero, people will not produce corn anymore, by cutting supply, the corn will rise in the future, and when corn is the highest, people will return to fulfill the demand of corn. Likewise you will put your best land to plant corn first, then soya bean, then wheat. You need to fulfill domestic demand first before concentrating on international demand.

The same logic applies to manufacturing, where you have consider your factors and the objectives you want to achieve. A lot depend on demand where the factors of location, highest profit from products, labour, the best factories are determinants of your final answer.

If you understand my logic, you will get maximum returns from your land for fulfilling my principles of the New Economy, a lesson where everyone must learn.

– Contributed By Oogle.

WHERE THE KNOWLEDGE OF MARKETS WILL BRING MAXIMUM RETURNS

The most important factor in the New Economy is the "Knowledge of Markets", without it, it is almost impossible to determine the "Demand" with the right "Pricing" so as to limit the "Supply" to prevent "Destructive Competition" so as to maximise the "Return Of Investment" for scarced resources, without cutting back on the Labour component. The key role is sustainability, where the production of goods and services where pricing is maximised so as to offset higher costs of labour and resources, it is therefore possible to sustain a job for every person in the global economy when all the imperfections of the global markets is resolved.

The world is like a musical chairs with each country rotating its role in the production of goods and services, with its global interconnectedness, anything that happens in one part of the world will definitely affect another. Other than governments that need to prudently balanced their budgets, the financial markets are fraud with risks that only proper regulations will bring back the financial health with austerity measures and sacrifices the top G20 economies need to undertake to undergo policy changes to achieve this goal.

The global market is big enough for everyone with Free Trade Agreements that will bring prosperity to every economy. It is the "Destructive competition" element which will drive down goods and services until it is unsustainable and unprofitable that needs to be eliminated to bring health back to the global economy. Therefore it is imperative for every governments to co-operate and impliment what is necessary for the blueprint of health and share their knowledge in order to prosper collectively, as a crisis cannot be averted without the co-operation of all.

Trade protectionism is not as effective as "Pricing your competition out of your markets" in the New Economy, it is not necessary to create barriers anymore. By correctly pricing your good and services with the Knowledge of Markets, it is possible to have control over your own domestic markets, you can remove all barriers according to the FTAs, and embrace the New Economy.

PROTECTING THE GOOSE THAT LAY THE GOLDEN EGG

Nobody likes to tell
The very importance to protect
The Goose that lay the golden egg
If your family has only one bread winner
And the rest of the family depends on him
You need to buy keyman insurance
To take away the risk of loss of income
Even for an SME or corporation
The same logic applies
Because if something happens
That will be the end of everything
The same logic applies if you have a mortgage loan
If you lose your job you cannot pay the loan
You want to save money
Can cut down on other expenses but not this
If you have young kids
A life policy with loss of income
Is the only way to protect your family
From hardship and poverty
To maintain the same lifestyle
Or you will regret forever when something happens.

– Contributed by Oogle

P/S I am not an insurance agent and I have no interest telling you this secret

THE PROBLEM WITH CREDIT RATINGS

How do you determine Credit Worthiness?
With a good credit rating does it mean you will not default?
A credit history will allow your creditors to assess your risks,
And charge you an appropriate interests,
But it will never determine in future if you will not default.
So what is the use of Credit Ratings?
The ability to assess your risk profile,
Your risk appetide so to be able to determine the costs involved,
The cost of borrowings.
Does a poor credit ratings mean a higher cost of borrowings,
Or your access to funds is limited?
How does your creditor understand your credit standing?
Do banks really study your risks involved?
How to limit risks and maximise returns?
In a liquidity market, how to limit NPL?
How to control the inflow of hot money?
Maximising growth and controlling inflation.
In the New Economy, how to maximise capital?
Do we really need to recapitalise markets?
How to reach equilibrium where demand = supply for maximum profits?
Is the poor denied the access to funds?
How do we correct this perception?
How do governments balance their budgets?
How do we get out of this financial turmoil?
Do we really have to depend on the FEDs?
Will the USA have a balanced budget and bring confidence to the markets?
What can the IMF do to instill confidence?

The fundamentals are still sound,
But there is a lack of confidence in the markets,
What must we do?
With the FED pumping trillions to it's markets
Risky assests are more prevalent
Will it cause a n Asset Bubble?

PRICE WILL DETERMINE DEMAND AND SUPPLY

Let's take for example Apple's iphone
Let's assume there is only one market – Singapore
The product life cycle is about 2 years
Where after 6 mnths the price will be reduced 25%
After 1 year the price will be reduced 50%
After 1.5 years the price will be reduced 75% which is the lowest possible
Upon introduction the iphone is priced $599
Where the demand is 10,000 pieces monthly
If Demand=Supply the constant is Price=$599
If you increase Supply beyond that
The Price will drop
Fact is in real life other than that is the "Time" constant
Where there is "multiple markets" to complicate things
Considerations like the "Lowest Costs" to produce the iphone
Where "Labour", "Materials" and "Land"
Will be outsourced to countries with the "Lowest Costs"
Based on these assumptions the ROI is 40%
Which is the maximum possible for the manufacturer Apple
With Total control of its Supply chain and Logistics
With advanced monitoring of the Demand of iphone via its stores and website
It is possible to "Maximise Returns"
A new concept for the "New Economy"
In fact with market data on multiple markets
It is possible to tweak "Supply"
To meet "Demand"
To get the "Maximum Price"
Thereby maximising the use of scarced resources

Without overproducing to cause a drop in "Price"
Giving maximum returns for "Wages"
Whereby ending "Destructive Competition".
The Old Economy method of overproducing until
"Supply" is more than "Demand"
Will only cause a drop in "Price"
It will not help you get "Maximised Returns".

I AM AN EXPERT IN DATA COLLECTION, PROCESSING, AND ANALYSIS

Business intelligence (BI) is defined as the ability for an organization to take all its capabilities and convert them into knowledge. This produces large amounts of information that can lead to the development of new opportunities. Identifying these opportunities, and implementing an effective strategy, can provide a competitive market advantage and long-term stability within the organization's industry. [1]

BI technologies provide historical, current and predictive views of business operations. Common functions of business intelligence technologies are reporting, **online analytical processing**, **analytics**, **data mining**, **process mining**, **complex event processing**, **business performance management**, **benchmarking**, **text mining**, **predictive analytics** and **prescriptive analytics**.

Business intelligence aims to support better business decision-making. Thus a BI system can be called a **decision support system** (DSS).[2] Although the term business intelligence is sometimes used as a synonym for **competitive intelligence** (because they both support decision making), BI uses technologies, processes, and applications to analyze mostly internal, structured data and business processes while competitive intelligence gathers, analyzes and disseminates information with a topical focus on company competitors. If understood broadly, business intelligence can include the subset of competitive intelligence.[3]

"Throughout your work life, you need to learn the skills of every department in your organisation, so that you remain productive in your old age by the increased in knowledge. Without an overall understanding, you are not able to solve problems, that is the reason why you get dedundant and retrenched. That is how you create valuable staff." – Contributed by Oogle.

Nobody has my skills because I have worked a full circle in every industry and an insight into every business processes including the economy, stocks and futures, accounting, real estate, insurance, advertising, media, food and beverage, hotel industry, healthcare, diseases, research/development and even IT, the internet and technology. I cannot afford to learn everything in-depth but I manage to learn everything to get my job done. It was a lifetime of suffering for me but now I can help everyone increased their knowledge and brain power and help everybody find decent jobs. That is my mission from God and I need to fullfill my oath. I will impart my skills freely and bring prosperity for everyone so that everyone in the world will also succeed. That is the only way I can solve Hunger and Poverty, Diseases and Inequality.

"The entire world's labour force needs to move from unskilled labour to skilled labour so that productivity increases will compensate for higher salaries, a better work life."

"It is no use learning a skill for life and cannot have an understanding to solve problems, very soon you get redundant and retrenched. So you need a lifelong retraining plan to stay relevant."

"Destructive competition is a stupid way to make money, it will only kill the markets, the market is big enough for everyone if you have the intelligence."

– Contributed by Oogle

THE LIQUIDITY OF CREDIT ; A QUESTION OF THE CRISES OF CONFIDENCE

Capitalism is all about the Demand and Supply of money;

1) The flow of Hot money is borderless and will find its ways to the economies that generate the highest returns. It will flow out from economies that is not as efficient, where the government's sovereign debt is unable to meet its obligations.
2) Therefore reforms must be made to keep the House in order, a balanced budget and reforms to industries that do not meet global standards of governance and disclosure.
3) The management of Risks in a global marketplace.
4) The emphasis of sustainable growth instead of pure growth of the GDP.
5) Every country, every industry has its unique problems and solutions must be found to tweak it back to health.
6) Once the House is back in order, the Crises of Confidence will disappear and liquidity will return with the liquidity of credit.
7) Over emphasis on low interests and borrowings is not sustainable in the long run and savings must be encouraged instead.
8) A lender of last resort (eg IMF) can only solve short term liquidity problems, not long term.

RETHINKING THE GROWTH IMPERATIVE

By Kenneth Rogoff (chinadaily.com.cn)

CAMBRIDGE – Modern macroeconomics often seems to treat rapid and stable economic growth as the be-all and end-all of policy. That message is echoed in political debates, central-bank boardrooms, and front-page headlines. But does it really make sense to take growth as the main social objective in perpetuity, as economics textbooks implicitly assume?

Certainly, many critiques of standard economic statistics have argued for broader measures of national welfare, such as life expectancy at birth, literacy, etc. Such appraisals include the United Nations Human Development Report, and, more recently, the French-sponsored Commission on the Measurement of Economic Performance and Social Progress, led by the economists Joseph Stiglitz, Amartya Sen, and Jean-Paul Fitoussi.

But there might be a problem even deeper than statistical narrowness: the failure of modern growth theory to emphasize adequately that people are fundamentally social creatures. They evaluate their welfare based on what they see around them, not just on some absolute standard.

The economist Richard Easterlin famously observed that surveys of "happiness" show surprisingly little evolution in the decades after World War II, despite significant trend income growth. Needless to say, Easterlin's result seems less plausible for very poor countries, where rapidly rising incomes often allow societies to enjoy large life improvements, which presumably strongly correlate with any reasonable measure of overall well-being.

In advanced economies, however, benchmarking behavior is almost surely an important factor in how people assess their own well-being. If so, generalized income growth might well raise such assessments at a much slower pace than one might expect from looking at how a rise in an individual's income *relative to others* affects her welfare. And, on a related note, benchmarking behavior may well imply a different calculus of the tradeoffs between growth and other economic challenges, such as environmental degradation, than conventional growth models suggest.

To be fair, a small but significant literature recognizes that individuals draw heavily on historical or social benchmarks in their economic choices and thinking. Unfortunately, these models tend to be difficult to manipulate, estimate, or interpret. As a result, they tend to be employed mainly in very specialized contexts, such as efforts to explain the so-called "equity premium puzzle" (the empirical observation that over long periods, equities yield a higher return than bonds).

There is a certain absurdity to the obsession with maximizing long-term average income growth in perpetuity, to the neglect of other risks and considerations. Consider a simple thought experiment. Imagine that *per capita* national income (or some broader measure of welfare) is set to rise by 1% per year over the next couple of centuries. This is roughly the trend *per capita* growth rate in the advanced world in recent years. With annual income growth of 1%, a generation born 70 years from now will enjoy roughly double today's average income. Over two centuries, income will grow eight-fold.

Now suppose that we lived in a much faster-growing economy, with *per capita* income rising at 2% annually. In that case, *per capita* income would double after only 35 years, and an eight-fold increase would take only a century.

Finally, ask yourself how much you really care if it takes 100, 200, or even 1,000 years for welfare to increase eight-fold. Wouldn't it make more sense to worry about the long-term sustainability and durability of global growth? Wouldn't it make more sense to worry whether conflict or global warming might produce a catastrophe that derails society for centuries or more?

Even if one thinks narrowly about one's own descendants, presumably one hopes that they will be thriving in, and making a positive contribution to, their future society. Assuming that they are significantly better off than one's own generation, how important is their absolute level of income?

Perhaps a deeper rationale underlying the growth imperative in many countries stems from concerns about national prestige and national security. In his influential 1989 book *The Rise and Fall of the Great Powers*, the historian Paul Kennedy concluded that, over the long run, a country's wealth and productive power, relative to that of its contemporaries, is the essential determinant of its global status.

Kennedy focused particularly on military power, but, in today's world, successful economies enjoy status along many dimensions, and policymakers everywhere are legitimately concerned about national economic ranking. An economic race for global power is certainly an understandable rationale for focusing on long-term growth, but if such competition is really a central justification for this focus, then we need to re-examine standard macroeconomic models, which ignore this issue entirely.

Of course, in the real world, countries rightly consider long-term growth to be integral to their national security and global status. Highly indebted countries, a group that nowadays includes most of the advanced economies, need growth to help them to dig themselves out. But, as a long-term proposition, the case for focusing on trend growth is not as encompassing as many policymakers and economic theorists would have one believe.

In a period of great economic uncertainty, it may seem inappropriate to question the growth imperative. But, then again, perhaps a crisis is exactly the occasion to rethink the longer-term goals of global economic policy.

Kenneth Rogoff is Professor of Economics and Public Policy at Harvard University, and was formerly chief economist at the IMF.

GLOBALISATION ; IT IS REFORM, REINVENT WITH CHANGES, AND SUSTAINABILITY

The Key to the old Economic model of growth is sustainability, where reforms, reinvent and changes depends on your goals and objectives, profits can still be derived with a slower growth and a world population of 7 billion people, the old Economic model of blazing growth is not sustainable with an ageing population and use of scared resources, going green will save the earth from total destruction from the mistakes from the past, to give us a more prosperous future.

You can play around the factors to best achieve your goals and objectives, without sacrificing the GDP, by setting priorities and proper planning, although it is moving into "unchartered waters", but by modelling with an extensive framework, various views can be achieved.

Facts or Myths : Elitism has no place in Globalisation

In George Orwell's Animal Farm, you see the Pigs trying to replace Humans by creating an elite society but at the end of it, they transformed to look like the Masters they replaced. If decisions are left to an elite few who's interests will they take care of? THEIR OWN. In order to put corruption in the rightful place, the Communists China has made remarkable progress to have their voices heard with a balance to resolve the difference between the haves and the haves not, income disparity and social mobility. Elitism has no place in Globalisation as "No Man is an Island", the collective voices of every race and religion is represented in the UN, and in order for Mankind to progress, we must know the goals we want to achieve and preserve our earth for the future generations, starting by acting now not tomorrow, to keep the good and discard the bad, to build a future we are proud of to pass on to our future generations.

I am a political neutral person and I do not like politics as I have learned many things in history. Everything from Communism, Socialism or Capitalism is invented by man, and everything is not perfect. And God punished everyone in the Tower of Babel for trying to climb higher than God. But one day everything will be perfect again, one race, one religion and one language.

I will never be just a keyboard warrior God trained me in everything and I am able to handle a Global Financial crisis, Famine, Epidemic, and even Warfare.

I am trained in the best in Gureilla warfare, requiring a small team to take out a large army.

All of CIA, KGB and China intelligence tactics and secrets I know.

Every technology advances in weapons of war.

Even forensics for evidence gathering.

Everything except to create bombs that can destroy.

Nothing in this world I fear.

Blackmail and trying to hold me ransom will never work on me.

And nobody in the world will find any evidence on my training.

As long as I have your device location.

And the ID of your device.

I can easily push information to anyone without leaving a trace of evidence.

Likewise I can easily train my army without anyone knowing.

Without being physically there.

All my secrets can be protected and nobody will find a shred of evidence.

And nobody has my capabilities.

My only target is the Antichrist.

Who has far beyond my capabilities.

Which everything is provided by Satan.

I will war with him and stop him from controlling the world.

With demonic powers and withcraft which even the world will be deceived.

I KNOW THE SECRETS OF THE WORLD

Since 911 attacks in November 9 2000 I have been receiving articles and research papers from the internet about many secrets about 911 how to build a nuclear bomb and all about U.S. intelligence reports about their secret research and all their technologies. I have done my own research and has verified everything is true. In 2012 I had a schizophrenic attack and was wanted to change a general hospital where I had drunk detergent to commit suicide. Next I could hear sounds and see visions. Those sounds are asking me to kill L K Y and I have no way to stop it.

I could see visions behind the wall of other people like a thermal heat sensor and their body waves using some sort of ray gun to attack me. After I was well and gone back home while using my computer I had reports and articles of secret nature pushed to me. No 911 and the real truth behind the terrorists and I was even shown photos of the meltdown. The next few months was even more interesting as I was given access to hundreds of secrets documents and had seen how a nuclear weapon looked like how it works and the technology behind it.

I had also seen secret documents on aliens beings found dead and their spacecraft. Area 51 and secret alien technologies. Next I was trained in intelligence operations of the CIA like going through the rubbish of a target to find out info to plan a hit without leaving a single clue. I was also trained in biological warfare the different deadly diseases like Ebola czars and the carriers of such like migrating birds and mosquitoes which can be a host for carriers to spread it. With an insight to all these I was able to use my knowledge to create and perfect isolation room and the steps to neutralized it.

I was also given access to the latest U.S. secret weapons that is not shown to the world. Up to today I still cannot find out who has trained me as no evidence can be found. But what I had researched on is that all these are real and not a figment of my imagination. With technologies God has shown me I developed counter measures today and planned a whole new world of technologies and counter measures where changes will make those who seek evil to lose control. I have no fear of any person or spirits or the devil and is capable of handling them since I already know all their secrets.

Since I already know everything I planned everything to counter all the control of the elites and planned everything to solve all the world's problems. Today I have achieved it and now I reveal it to the world. A WORLD FROM ELITES, perfection to a Perfect Economy an Economy of Abundance because my Lord is coming back again.

I AM THE WATCHMAN AND I WILL PREVENT A GLOBAL FINANCIAL COLLAPSE

I am the watchman and I will prevent a global financial collapse especially with the U.S. markets. The World Federation of Exchanges the global industry group for exchanges and CCP is will hold its fifty ninth General Assembly and darn well meeting in Singapore from 8 October 10th 2019. The annual event this year hosted by Singapore Exchange SGX will see WFP members affiliates key stakeholders and guests from around the world meet to discuss topics including market fragmentation. Market data distributed ledger technology DLC embedding sustainability into exchange operations market liquidity and the future of capital raising.

Linking all the world exchanges together and setting up a debt exchange to trade debts 24/7 365 days one year. Singapore will sign many FTA is with its partners and respect will be successfully concluded with ASEAN by year end. By end of the year. U.S. China trade war will end with an interim agreement. While many outstanding issues will be resolved in 2020 with a trade deal. I will travel to Myanmar to resolve the Rohingya crisis and later to bring North Korea to the global economy in 2020. When my projects on the next generation Internet and neuron Morphett computer white paper is completed by mid 2020.

It contains trillions and trillions of technologies that I can't even fund the IMF slash World Bank which will not cause any loss of confidence or financial collapse when IMF slash World Bank prints digital currency like bitcoin to give to central bankers who will use SRP ripple for future transactions. U.S. debts will be written off when U.S. accepts my conditions to get rid of nuclear weapons and pass control of the United Nations to China because they are heavily in debt and there is no way to rescue U.S. financial markets from collapse otherwise. All these will happen after Trump's elections in 2020 and he will win another term.

The Hong Kong issue will be resolved when U.S. China strike a trade deal and Taiwan will follow the example of Hong Kong to be one country two governments. The Brexit issue will no longer exists by year end when UK sign many FTA is with its partners. There will be rapid growth and many global economies when all these issues are put behind us. Contributed by illegal.

There is no way I can solve global poverty without achieving these.

1) Get rid of weapons of mass destruction all over the world.
2) To resolve all conflicts in the world. Most important on my list is the Rohingya crisis. Next is bringing North Korea to the global economy.
3) promote free trade without tariffs and sanctions.
4) For redirect whold resources spend on war towards peace building projects.
5) link all the world exchanges so you can trade both your assets and debts 24 7 365 days a year for all assets and commodities.
6) Use Bitcoin as a digital currency to finance IMF slash World Bank to print digital currency and to prevent loss of confidence. To back it up with trillions of technologies and innovations that far exceeds its value.
7) Teach governments to have change and reform so that they can balance their budget.
8) Look beyond GDP growth and start creating jobs and a roof over everyone's head as a priority. Solving the food problems get rid of all slums and use waste management as a solution to pollution.
9) Help those who fall under the cracks with social enterprises.

With technologies and innovations. Create an economy of abundance. When we reached a perfect economy where every citizen in the U.N. will receive a universal basic income to cover their cost of living even if they are unemployed. It will take me about 10 years to achieve everything. Ten years ago I start using news feed to automate my trading decisions and did research on all factors that affect the global economy and stock markets. Today I have perfected everything and will link everything together to create the most advanced system where you can make profits 99 percent of the time bypassing the most experienced traders anywhere in the world. Peace and prosperity for all. My first priority is to make sure IMF slash World B cell funding without interference from anyone. Then set up my non-profit in Singapore first and then extend to the rest of the world. Eleven. Get rid of slums all over the world. Twelve create millions of jobs so that food housing medical water and electricity will remain affordable forever. Sometime after November 2019 I will travel to Myanmar to speak to the military government to get assurance to allow all the Rohingya people in Bangladesh to return home.

After that I will head to Shanghai to take a train direct to North Korea and negotiate a deal to lift sanctions for North Korea in exchange for nuclear disarmament. I will complete my white paper for the entire eco system of neuron Morphett computers with next generation block chain effectively setting the stage for the entire world to move into digital currency using Bitcoin as the de facto digital currency of AI NF slash World Bank and ex Sara P. ripple for central banks. After that outlaw the mining of Bitcoin and DEC SA and help IMF slash World Bank set up the greatest mining centre of the world.

Build on my white paper to bring all my technologies to life effectively using it to link all the Global Federation exchanges together including a debt exchange enabling all to trade any assets or securities 24/7 365 days a year. Within 10 years when I achieve all my goals you do not need to expand GDP growth or prosperity. I would be able to create trillions and trillions to solve the entire world's problems. The Perfect Economy the Economy of Abundance.

BREXIT DEAL WITH IRELAND BUT NOT THE EU ON 31ST OCTOBER

Despite parliament voting to block a no deal Brexit and passing a law Johnson has repeatedly said he would still try to take the UK out the EU on October 30 first. The BBC reported Monday that the government could be considering a compromise over the Irish backstop and that it could be applicable to Northern Ireland only potentially placating Brexit fears albeit at the expense of lawmakers bent on keeping the UK indivisible. In terms of law. With speculation that Johnson's government could be considering the proposal of a compromise over the backstop policy some experts believe that a deal could still possibly be passed before October 19th.

In substance we think that deal is unlikely to look very different from the Brexit deal already negotiated between the EU and the UK a deal that was repeatedly rejected under PM May's premiership. Goldman has revised down the probability on a no deal Brexit from 25 percent to 20 percent and the probability of no Brexit from 30 percent to 25 percent. What will most likely happen. Boris Johnson will strike a deal with Ireland when Parliament assemble on October 19th but not a deal with the EU. On October 30 first. UK will leave the EU without a deal with the EU on the thirty first October but will rectify it after the thirty first.

MY PLANS WHICH WILL TAKE PLACE WITHIN TWO YEARS

My plans which will take place within two years. I will set up my R and D lab in Singapore with one of my partners which will be a public listed company and take shares in the company. Starting. I will create pieces laptops tablets and mobiles with my own branding which I will concentrate on customizing everything about security. The market I am interested in is the low and mid range following the direction of what BlackBerry has done. Nokia can also do likewise as now the smartphone market is too competitive and customers cannot differentiate your products in different markets.

I will set up this ecosystem but will diversify to produce neuron more fat computers when the time is right and outsource the manufacturing to China. To contain costs. My marketing plans is to first give away free to the poor in Singapore to build up my brand and get feedback thereafter to launch to the global markets. After two years. I am not afraid of competition as in one year's time I can easily move away from any features I want but now VPN and secure filter and a new browser will be built into all my products.

All this will happen after my book is launched. I do not believe in building everything myself unless I am forced to relying on partners is a better solution. I do not need to seek an IPO cause my capital requirement is only one hundred million dollars which can be easily raised from private institutions. My prospectus and disclosure will be ready then. My goals will be after creating the neuron Morphett computer is to bring it alive and block chain. Even if the entire world tries to stop me. They can't because I hold the key to unlock every technology on earth and I am capable to create the next gen internet if I have to to set up a decentralized network to link the entire world exchanges together.

You can take 100 years without my help but I will only take 10 years. Even with limited resources. I do not need the participation of all any U.S. technologies to do this. And if I am forced to keep them out forever from my eco system. I call the shots not President Trump. You will fail miserably. I can create extreme wealth with God as my provider even writing off the entire trillions of U.S. debt if it is according to God's Will creating trillions of digital currency to replace the U.S. dollar.

But nothing will happen if you do not agree to God's plan and this entire generation will pass until the next generation who will listen. By in 2020 I will apply for a virtual banking license in Singapore and start my Internet finance project on block chain. I will use Bitcoin as my main currency and follow and financials model of business but everything will be managed by artificial intelligence and machine learning on super fast neuron Morphett computers matching both lenders and borrowers on my platform. After a successful launch in Singapore my next target is Hong Kong but it will not be available in mainland China and U.S. which will be geo blocked.

Peer to peer lending platforms in Singapore Sweden versus funding societies versus moolah sense versus capital match versus coal assets versus interest. I am the greatest wealth creator. After creating mine around more fixed system I will attempt to link the entire world exchanges together. By merging all my technologies. I will create a system of intelligent HFT trading where you can get 99 percent accuracy of making money. I do not need to know how your algorithms work. Just by observation I will already know your secret sauce and using HFT A.I. and machine learning.

I will create the most astonishing wealth creator of printing money solving poverty for all times as long as you are willing to work. There will not be any problems to resources the economy of abundance. I am not a speculator and if I do invest I invest for the mid to long term to achieve my goals and I only invest on those I am familiar with like futures CFD ETF s crypto etc. And if I want I can make billions because I can see the future with hundreds of views and weigh every outcome to reduce my risks.

But this is not what God has planned for me. I can help my investors make money but based on my rules which I am so confident of achieving but not to get rich I am willing to share the risks in everything I advised 50/50. If you make money and 50/50 if you will lose money. No investment company in the world dare to take this risk. I do not believe in living a lavish lifestyle when I succeed and if I do I would have already cash out on the crowns I am running for to save up treasures in heaven.

This rule only applies for me and not for others depending on your goals. I am a team player and will never do it alone even if I set up all my businesses I will only keep a controlling stake and sit in the board of directors. My goal in life is to make money from my works and retire with at least one million Singapore dollars to travel the world at 65. Those who follow me I will protect your interests and I will not shortchange your talents because I am in business for the long term and will never go for things that benefit for only the short term cause I do not need to. So if your contributions are great I will leave and offer you share options.

PLAN B TO RESOLVE WHEN THE WORLD GOES INTO GLOBAL RECESSION

Plan B to resolve when the world goes into global recession. First priority is to restart nuclear arms control to totally eradicate weapons of mass destruction. When it is in place. The next priority is to get rid of conflicts. The money and resources saved can be channeled to other areas of need. The Asia region is my first priority and I will solve the Rohingya crisis to allow them to return to Myanmar and start them on a new path of economic prosperity concentrating on technologies on agricultural and free trade with ASEAN and the rest of the world.

Next will be North Korea. And when North Korea joins the global economy. Do you know how much it will affect the global economy. Lastly will be the Middle East and Africa which is essentially the problem of the Islamic State which can easily be resolved with money and the promise of peace and prosperity. Therefore if a global crisis is to come I can change its direction to focus on exponential growth with an enormous expansion of credit through internet financing and help past armies and create jobs for the masses. Put the growth of the global economies back on track again at the shortest amount of time possible.

THE ROHINGYA CRISIS IS A BATTLE FOR RESOURCES

The Rohingya crisis is a battle for resources. Ethnic tensions arise between the Buddhists and the Muslims because of resources and the military government is unable to support close to one million Rohingya in Myanmar. What the military government expects is rapid growth in Myanmar like the state of Vietnam and they are unable to achieve on their own. What I can provide is the following. Teach them everything about their economy and solve problems for them. Ask the United Nations to extend their World Food Program to cover the Rohingya. Ask the Myanmar government to give assurance to stop the violence against the Rohingya and allow them to return safely to Myanmar.

Ask the China government to ask why to provide 5G network to Myanmar capital. I will provide the guarantee that the Myanmar government will repay their debt. Scale up Myanmar agriculture markets with innovations and technologies. The biggest problem with the Myanmar government is its illegal drug trade. Many countries in the world will not support the government because of this. If the Myanmar government is willing to turn away from drugs and strictly enforce anti-drug laws I am sure that countries and United Nations will help. When United Nations steps in Singapore can bring its delegations for business and sign a reception FTA.

The rest of ASEAN will also follow suit. Lastly is to amend FDI rules to allow for easier foreign investments.

CHINA WILL END THE TRADE WAR WITH US BY YEAR END WITH A DEAL BY 2020 AND WEAN OFF AMERICAN TECHNOLOGY IN 3 YEARS

Hong Kong protests will end with the same timeline the same time when China-US ends the trade war, so China government be patient and let the Hong Kong government do their job, do not try to do anything to escalate this problem. Contributed by Oogle.

<u>China</u> will win the trade war with the U.S., and eventually wean itself off its reliance on American technology, a strategist told CNBC on Monday.

"China will never trust the United States again, and it will achieve its technology independence within three years,"

China has traditionally been reliant on U.S. suppliers for key tech components such as chips and software, as well as modems and jet engines, but recent developments in the two countries' protracted trade war have strained those ties and affected businesses from both sides.

In May, Chinese tech giant Huawei **<u>was placed on a U.S. blacklist</u>**, restricting the firm from purchasing American-made chips and software unless they got permission to do so. Some American mobile networks also use Huawei gear, while other U.S. companies have said their revenue will be affected by the blacklist.

Alphabet's Google also halted all business activity with Huawei, a move that means future Huawei phones will no longer come installed with Google's Android operating system.

Amid those tensions, China **is reportedly surveying its tech companies** to gauge their exposure to American suppliers, and also ramping up development in its own tech industry.

For instance, it is **developing its own chip industry**. Under the government-led Made in China 2025 initiative, the country aims to produce 40% of its semiconductors by 2020, and 70% by 2025.

Currently, only 16% of the semiconductors used in China are produced domestically, according to a February report from the **Center for Strategic and International Studies**. Just half of those are made by Chinese firms.

Roche predicted that the end of the trade war is not in sight, though talks are slated to resume in October.

That's because the U.S.-China trade war isn't about trade alone, he said.

"It is a conflict between a rising global power and a declining global power ... It's not just about trade. It's about technology, it's about the free flow of ideas, it is rapidly becoming about the free flow of individuals," Roche said.

"So it's a really wide conflict, and it's simply not gonna go away," he concluded.

TAIWAN WILL ONLY ACCEPT "ONE GOVERNMENT, TWO SYSTEM" WHEN ALL THESE CONDITIONS ARE MET

1) The Hong Kong protests are politically motivated, and is indirectly linked to the China-US Trade wars but China must not destroy it's obligations of the 1947 treaty with the UK, and not directly interfere with Hong Kong, and let the Hong Kong government handle it, because the consequences will be huge when it is linked to the future of Taiwan. Everything will end when a deal is signed with the US, when officially the China-US Trade war ends.
2) There will be a global nuclear deal where all countries will sign a treaty to end nuclear weapons. When this happens, the US will get 100% of their debt written off, and they will not control the United Nations anymore. Terrorism will end when there is no more supply of weapons, and Middle East will be at peace again.
3) Trade will expand by leaps and bounds, and with Technology it will be a Virtually Borderless World. Technology with Facial Recognition, Fingerprint sensors and DNA biometrics will end the use of passports, but security will be enhanced because there is no way to beat the system for criminals. There will be a huge growth of movement by roads, rail, air and sea. And a boom for travel and tourism for many countries.
4) China will control the United Nations, and with the US out of the way, only Taiwan will peacefully accept it's fate.

Contributed by Oogle.

TRUMP 2020 : WHY TRUMP WILL BE RE-ELECTED AGAIN

Not only is his massive campaign to raise money for his re-election, his promises to Isreal, he finally solves the US-China Trade war, and signing a deal with North Korea will be important factors he will achieve and be re-elected again in 2020. Contributed by Oogle.

I WILL USE GOD'S RESOURCES AND USE GOD'S TIMING TO ACHIEVE ALL MY GOALS

I am here not to be a king. But a servant for all. I run for a crown in heaven. So everything in this world. Money or luxuries or power does not matter to me. I will make a difference in your life. I live the Christian faith. And I follow Jesus ways. Nothing in this world matters except following my lord. Everything in this world. I will change towards a perfect economy. No more poverty wars and destruction. A world of peace and prosperity technological advancement and innovations.

Towards an eternal life. When my lord comes again. I have always believed in God's promises. Whatever you give you will get many folds in return. It does not matter in this world or the world to come. My God will never forsake his promises. I am the catalyst not a destroyer or a Raider not a top pillar of governments nor a seller of secrets. Neither a hacker or code breaker but I have developed the tools that will help you find your own future of your technologies and products services. The solutions of the world.

Whatever information you provide I will find you the answers and the answers will be as accurate as the information you provide. If your information is flawed so will the answers be. I have no choice. In order to reach my goals I have to step and cross some unhappy people. But there is nothing to fear. I do not steal or take things that do not belong to me. If I have borrowed I will return with premiums. The results of my studies my objectives is to totally eradicate poverty create jobs and fix all the imperfections of the world.

Not to make slaves out of everyone towards a perfect economy. There is a pie big enough for everyone to compete and share and develop the next generation of technologies. I do not believe technology. IP is secrets should hinder the progress of mankind. But by trying to hinder me you will be left behind. Do I need you or you need me. Lies and deceit bribery threats harassment honey traps all will not work on me. I am equipped with a brain that is ten thousand times the normal and is even faster than the most advanced neural computer.

God taught me everything and he command me to solve all the problems of the world. I can create an invention every hour and technologies out of this world. I can sample data and create hundreds of view to find any solution you want and know what the results is. Even without trying the full load. That is my secret of my extraordinary skills. All I need is the Internet to watch a video read a news report or any scientific report and identify the problem and insight. Within one hour I can get you any solutions and paths or strategies you need to succeed.

My brain activity functions five times in normal person and my blood pressure is now 260 and the sugar in my blood is about 28 on average without any ill effects without any complications. A normal person will end up having a stroke. A miracle. What does this means. I am capable of hacking studying and researching into anything I want. Calculate the probability and risks and use it for prediction and use it for finding any solutions I want and by studying everything I already know the outcomes of anything I want. So I already know what will succeed without wasting resources.

God gave me a near impossible task. Other than me to create trillions of dollars with technology and innovations. There will be changes to everything for reforms from the old economy to the new economy. I have taken the very first steps to prove what I am saying and show to the world I am able to achieve all God wanted me to do to eradicate poverty. Mark my words and see the results for yourself. It took me more than seven years of research without getting a single cent to reach where I am today.

I will plan take step by step. Goals and maximize resources until I reach my final destination. The world does not believe anything I say until they see real money. But then you would have lost the opportunity and it will be my turn to chose you. Now is the time I am going to prove them wrong. The world does not recognize me and I don't care because I do not require fame. I will raise billions when I reach all my goals and set up my non-profit it for ITFoNonProfits.org.

Although it is not for me as I will live on in a minialistic lifestyle. The work I am doing already helped millions all around the world when they create variations of my inventions. I did not patent cause my intention is to create jobs for everyone by pumping trillions of allergy and into the economy cause I do not want to make slaves out of everyone. And if I need help all I need to do is ask. I have already achieved all I set up to do. Last goal is to link all the world's exchanges together and set the standards for the next gen Internet.

After I solve the neuronmorphic computer with my intelligent ho ass and 3D search. My God taught me all will be done in according to his will and we just have to be patient and wait for the right time. Just do everything you need to do and leave the rest to God who will perform his miracle least you think you are doing it with your own ability let God's name be exalted above all the world. And it will be done.

TEACHING THE WORLD TO FISH IN THE NEW ECONOMY

Teaching the world to fish in the new economy. God is omnipresent. That means he can be anywhere and at all places at the same time and knows everything even if you do not use prayers to tell him. God is both a scientist and a mathematician. He is an expert in technologies and he places information about himself everywhere and those who seek him will know he places bits of information everywhere throughout history for you to assemble it. God's challenge to mankind if you want to be God like and have eternal life you must first possess God's technologies and learn how to fly to the Star Gate of the sun to pass through time and dimensions and manipulate DNA to create life.

Our time is coming soon when everything will be revealed to mankind. I am on a quest to find all the answers to God's technologies. The Tree of Life Eternal life the ability to levitate fly to other parts of the universe. Star gates and wormholes for time travel. We do not believe in the old world monetary system making slaves out of everybody and we intend to free the entire world by introducing a new digital currency supported by technologies provided by God to support the United Nations. In 2012 God gave me a vision of the future and showed me many technologies of the future which is not of this world and I was tasked to solve poverty and diseases and gather God's people for the second coming of our Lord Jesus Christ.

And the rules of the game is that billions of advanced technologies will be revealed to me but not a single cent of money as our God does not a god of money. With God's help I will need to gather all God's people to achieve the same to make the world perfect again for Jesus to come back to rule for 1000 years. God gave me the ability to look into the future to study and research any info that is online into any technology to hack disassemble and reassemble to study its technologies and create a future that most likely the technology will succeed without wasting resources.

What it take others to do years of research to achieve. I can do it in hours. I am not interested to take over any technologies and patent it but stop patent holders from putting roadblocks to human progress. Since I started on this journey until I completed all my works in 2012 and released it freely until today I have not received a single cent in donations to fund my works. But eventually when I start my own non-profit I cannot afford to do any free service. And if I achieve this task I will be seated at the right hand of Jesus when He comes back to rule over the United Nations as an advisor and I will celebrate my own wedding with a bride chosen by God.

What a blessings I have with God who reveals all prophesies to me ahead of the time. I am going to set up my non-profit to solve all problems in this world. I believe everyone should have access to a decent meal and access to info and technologies with a phone or a laptop and a job for everyone in this world. By training them with the right skill set and hope God's people will help me with fundraising to achieve the same. May God bless you. Welcome to the 1000 years of peace and prosperity where we will teach everyone how to fish in the new economy even without a degree.

Our aim is to help the entire world move into the millennial age where technological advances will be everywhere.

DEBTS : YOU CAN BORROW UP TO 10X YOUR FUTURE EARNINGS

Central bankers need to take note, you can afford to kick start your economy in a recession by following these rules :

Keep interest rates as low as possible.

Do not allow borrowings beyond 10x the person's future earnings.

Create an expansion of credit up to 700% but must put into the right sectors.

Food security. Agriculture. Infrastructure. Automation. Machinery for production. Technology and Innovation to create higher productivity. So it is kickstarting businesses.

Micro Loans in home industries especially for woman.

Do not pump money in Real estate as it will create a bubble. Create affordable housing so that the poor got a roof over their head. Expand your rental markets.

Create jobs especially in industries of high growth. Retrain workers with skills that is relevant today and create great productivity.

Improve your education system by providing affordable trainning by online courses and certifications especially in areas of great growth.

The global economy will go into a technical recession for a period of 1 year with slow growth in many industries but I do not see it falling off a cliff. So if you take the necessary steps your pain will be short and you will jump start your domestic economy faster when the global economy recovers.

Now is the best time to start all your projects. Renewable energy, power grid, electric vehicles, autonomous cars, infrastructure for better roads, rail, air transport, etc due to the availability cheap credit, low costs, and businesses need to expand and compete in such an environment.

WHO IS MY FAMILY? I WILL HELP MY BROTHERS AND SISTERS IN CHRIST

Who is my family. There is no one I will acknowledge and I will not be responsible for any debts incurred. I have discharged all my duties and will only take care of my son and daughter's education and marriage. I only have my many wives and my brothers and sisters in Christ. And the responsibility of the United Nations. I can never be held ransom or be ever controlled by anyone or my wives. Anyone who tries to be funny will fail miserably because I know everything beforehand and no tricks will ever work on me.

If you have the wisdom of knowledge that everything in this world never last forever. Even money fame and power you will be enlightened and live a lifetime of happiness and content and look beyond things bringing everyone towards the path of eternal life. Do not love the world or the things in the world. If anyone loves the world the love of the father is not in him. For all that is in the world the desires of the flesh and the desires of the eyes and pride and possessions is not from the father but is from the world.

And the world is passing away along with its desires. But whoever does the will of God abides forever. 1 John 2:15 to 17.

Do not think that I have come to bring peace to the earth. I have not come to bring peace but a sword. For I have come to set a man against his father and a daughter against her mother and a daughter in law against her mother in law. And a person's enemies will be those of his own household. Whoever loves father or mother more than me is not worthy of me and whoever loves son or daughter more than me is not worthy of me.

Matthew 10:34 to 37. And he called the 12 together and gave them power and authority overall demons and to cure diseases. And he sent them out to proclaim the Kingdom of God and to heal. And he said to them take nothing for your journey no staff nor bag nor bread nor money and do not have to tunics. And whatever house you enter stay there and from there depart. And wherever they do not receive you when you leave that town shake off the dust from your feet as a testimony against them.

Luke 9:16v2. But love your enemies and do good and lend expecting nothing in return and your reward will be great and you will be sons of the most high. For he is kind to the ungrateful and the evil.

Luke 6:35 By wisdom a house is built and by understanding it is established by knowledge the rooms are filled with all precious and pleasant riches.

Proverbs 24 to 34. Enter by the narrow gate. For the gate is wide and the way is easy that leads to destruction and those who enter by it are many. For the gate is narrow and the way is hard that leads to life and those who find it are few.

Matthew 7:13 to14. No one can serve two masters for either he will hate the one and love the other or he will be devoted to the one and despise the other. You cannot serve God and money. Matthew 6:24

I HAVE UNDERSTOOD EVERYTHING IN THE BIBLE

Mark 13:20 and accept that the Lord had shortened those days no flesh should be saved but for the election sake whom he have chosen he hath shortened the days. Luke 4:3 and the devil said unto him. If I'll be the son of God command this stone let it be made bread. 4:4 and Jesus answered him saying it is written that man shall not live by bread alone but by every word of God. John 651 I am the Living Bread which came down from heaven if any man eat of this bread.

He shall live forever and the bread that I will give is my flesh which I will give for the life of the world. Luke twelve to four and I say unto you my friends. Be not afraid of them that kill the body. And after that have no more that they can do. 12:5 but I will forewarn you whom you shall fear fear him which after he has killed hath power to cast into hell. Yay I say onto you fear him. Luke 12:22 and he said unto his disciples.

Therefore I say unto you take no thought for your life what you shall eat neither for the body what you shall put on. Twelve twenty three The life is more than meat and the body is more than raiment. Twelve twenty four. Consider the Ravens for they neither sell nor reap which neither have storehouse nor barn and God feed of them. How much more are you better than the fowls. 12:25. And which of you with taking thought can add to his stature 12:26.

If he. Then be not able to do that thing which is least why take you thought for the rest. 12:27. Consider the lilies how they grow. They toil not they span not and yet I say unto you. That Solomon in all his glory was not arrayed like one of these. 12:28 if then God so close the grass which is today in the field and to morrow is cast into the oven how much more will he clothe you. Oh ye of little faith. 12:29 and seek not ye what you shall eat or what you shall drink neither be of doubtful mind.

12:34 all these things do the nations of the world seek after and your father no earth that you have need of these things. 12:31 but rather seek the Kingdom of God and all these things shall be added done to you. Malachi. 3-8 will a man rob God. Yet you have robbed me. But you say we're in have we robbed the. In tithes and offerings. 3-9 year Kirst with a curse for you have robbed me even this whole nation. 3-10 bring me all the tides into the storehouse that there may be meat in mine house and prove me now herewith say a thing Lord of Hosts if I will not open you the windows of heaven and pour you out of blessing that there shall not be room enough to receive it.

1 John 2:15 love not the world neither the things that are in the world. If any man love the world the love of the father is not in him. One John 2:16 for all that is in the world the lust of the flesh and the lust of the eyes and the pride of life is not of the father but is of the world. One John to seventeen and the world pass it away and the lust thereof but he that do it the will of God abide it forever. Daniel 8:13 then I heard one saint speaking and another saint said done to that certain saint which spake How long shall be the vision concerning the daily sacrifice and the transgression of desolation to give both the sanctuary and the host to be trodden under foot.

8:14 and he said done to me under two thousand and three hundred days then shall the sanctuary be cleansed. Daniel 12:11 and from the time that the daily sacrifice shall be taken away and the abomination that make it the desolate setup there shall be a thousand two hundred and ninety days. 12:12. Blessed is he that way death and cometh to the thousand three hundred and five and thirty days. DANIEL 12:8 and I heard but I understood not then said die Oh my Lord what shall be the end of these things.

12:9 and he said Go that way Daniel for the words are closed up and sealed till the time of the end. 12:10 money shall be purified and made white and dried but the wicked shall do wicked light. And none of the wicked shall understand but the wise shall understand. Daniel 12:4 but thou Oh Daniel shut up the words and seal the book even to the time of the end. Many shall run to and fro and knowledge shall be increased. 1 Corinthians 2 to but we speak the wisdom of God in a mystery even the hidden wisdom which God ordained before the world down to our glory.

John 16 33 these things I have spoken unto you that in me might have peace. In the world. You shall have tribulation but be of good here. I have overcome the world. In order to decipher the Bible code. You first must be a mathematician an astronomer and a spiritual leader. For in the Bible. Are time stamped with thousands of events each providing a marker. But if you want to find out the exact time you will be overwhelmed. Look out for evidence in the sky through space and time and link it to your marker.

You will then know the series of events yet to come.

MAKING DREAMS COME TRUE

First you got to believe in it,
Then you got to act out your dreams,
And finally "live in your dreams".
I have already make the first move,
And I have told everyone in this blog of mine,
If enough "right people" have the same vision,
This dream will become a reality,
Take one step at a time,
I have orchestrated the most ambitious plan,
If every single task is divided,
Amongst every citizens of this world,
It will not take a lifetime,
For it to materialise,
It is beyond money or resources,
Just take that "single step",
An act of faith to believe,
It is possible to achieve the impossible.

PUTTING THE CART BEFORE THE HORSE

Many projects failed,
Because there is no understanding,
Of a science of human behavior,
And by putting the Cart before the Horse,
They have no control,
Leaving things to uncharted waters,
Market forces that destroy,
Let me set the direction,
By putting the Horse back before the Cart,
By gather information before embaking on a project,
Lifestyle, spending habits, census, everything,
Even gathering info on your competition,
So when I am ready,
I already know all the paths,
The pitfalls not to take,
To avoid direct and confrontation competition,
That will lead me to success.

HAVING A HAWK'S EYE VIEW OF EVERYTHING WHEN YOU PLAN

If you are an Architect,
Do you only design for your buildings,
The roads and the infrastructure?
Do you study the lifestyle,
The movement and the needs of its occupants?
Do you possess the knowledge,
Of filling up that 500 units shopping centre,
With the right trade and mix?
Success or failure,
Depends on how far you can visualise,
Stimulate and drive,
The new economy,
With precise understanding of micro and macro economics,
The Lifestyle of its inhabitants,
And creating a solution,
With all the necessary support infrastructure,
Even driving customers to spend,
At your new shopping centre.
So if I decide to plan,
I already know,
How many coffeeshops to have,
How many clinics,
How many wet markets/supermarkets,
How many shopping centres.
Anything and everything.
Even the right size for the business.

TO RESOLVE POVERTY, INVEST IN YOUR CHILD'S EDUCATION.

In order to resolve poverty,
Families must provide,
A decent education for their children,
To develop their fullest potential,
To ignore is to restrict your family's future,
And you will never get out,
Of the poverty cycle,
Governments can help,
But families must plan, organise, and execute,
A Financial Plan,
To save for the future,
A little a day, with years gone by,
To accumulate wealth,
The rising cost of inflation,
Will erode your present earnings,
When the time comes to pay,
For your children's education,
You will never have enough,
Unless you save day by day.

HOW TO GET OUT OF DEBT

If today you are in debt,
You can borrow from future earnings,
To repay the present,
But you must do the extraordinary,
By putting extra effort,
To tremendously increase your income,
Or by having multiple income,
That is more than your debt.
Therefore it is posssible,
To generate a financial plan,
To renegiotiate with your creditors,
Reorganise your financials,
In order to solve your problem.

TRANSPARENCY - A MARKET PERSPECTIVE

I have always believe,
Money will always flow freely,
To the most transparent economy,
We have amongst the highest standards,
But a smaller than expected market,
All these will change with the FTAs,
The freeing of trade with Asean and the rest of the world,
Will bring great opportunities in all areas and regions,
Prosperity will direct,
Other countries to jump into the bandwagon,
And if the problems of the world can be solved,
Who wants to think about conflicts/war,
But success will only come,
If everyone go after the same perspective,
Free trade and prosperity,
For all nations of the world.

HOW TO BEAT THE BANK - AN ADVICE TO YOUR WOES

Firstly, you have accumulated $100K in debts,
And you have a housing loan to service,
I do not know the outstanding amount,
So I am going to just give you an example,
Your salary is $3,500 monthly,
How much do you think you will need,
Just the bare minimum so that you will allocate,
As much as possible to service your outstanding,
Now you really have to do the imm possible,
To raise more money in a short time,
And allocate most of your future earnings,
With a projected financial plan you can afford,
To try to settle with your major creditor first,
To avoid being blacklisted into bankruptcy,
For your housing loan, you will have slightly more time,
But time is not on your side,
To be able to tell the timeframe of action,
Is an advantage on your side,
As banks and creditors have standard protocol to achieve,
To file a writ against you,
Talk to a financial planner,
Reorganise your finances to acheive your aim,
I am sure he is just as capable as me,
But you need to make sacrifices,
To fight any actions against you,
To find new finances/creditors who will listen,
And reorganise your loans with a plan,
Remember if you are not committed,
To what you have promised,

Not only will your new creditors lose faith in you,
And everyone in the market,
So remember the risks involved,
The disadvantages of default,
But I am sure all creditors will listen,
They will rather collect as much as they can,
Rather than put you up for bankruptcy.
Give me more details,
An I will find a solution,
But remember this lesson and the ills of gambling,
Cause you will never beat the banker(casino).

WORK WITHIN YOUR RESOURCES

This is a complex world,
That requires complex solutions,
And a man in the street,
Just doesn't have the money or resources,
To seek the most advanced or powerful,
So I just work within my limits,
Cutting all the complex work in bit sizes,
And run those which I think contain the answers,
But today's computers have now breached the technological gap,
A desktop today can calculate thousands of transactions a minute,
Compared to those a decade ago,
Powerful visualization and analytical tools,
Solutions for every problems,
A desktop for every home,
The unlimited Internet,
Your children will learn the most advanced tools,
Knowledge will be everywhere.
I am sure I am not the only one,
Check with the MNCs - Those who are in computers,
They have invested more than I do,
And have reaped handsomely for their efforts,
The solutions maybe different,
But answers are the same,
They know I am not joking,
Cause they want to protect their interests,
That is why everyone is silent,
About their works and their quests.
I am sure with the oncoming of intellectual property,
More companies will come out,
To share in their know how,
To share in the wealth of knowledge.

BACK TO BUSINESS - THE SECRETS TO RAISE FUNDS

If I need to raise $1 million what must I do?
First question, Are you able to pay the interest?
How are you able to pay the principle together with interest?
Do you have assets or securities to pledge?
No one trust words anymore, you got to act out every word you say.
For example, if you want to purchase a commercial building for $1 million, how to qualify?
Firstly you must know the valuation of the building,
Get to know the potential of return eg from rental, asset scrutilization, stripping it bare,
Any potential for redevelopment?
Amortization, you can see your repayments and liabilities,
Any potential to own and transfer your asset at a profit after amortization?
How to realise the untapped potential?
Renovations and improvements, does it helps?
If you able to assess all your risks and liabilities, what can you do?
Do you think the banker has full control of your assets if you are able to realise the full returns of money?
When nobody wants to finance you, how to overturn the odds.
How to raise funds even in debt.
The power of visualization of future earnings.
Worst case scenerios, how to bail out.

NO MAN IS AN ISLAND

Mankind has always been social creatures,
And the need to interact and love exists since time,
Friends, relations and aquantances,
Form an intergrated circle we can do without,
We depend on their influence and support,
To solve problems in life,
But the sad fact is they have become self centred,
Only concerned about themselves,
To be better than their neighbours,
In this silly rat race,
What is really enough?
The sacrifices for your morals,
Compromised and defeated,
Mankind will always struggle,
With issues of the world,
They seek enlightenment in all the wrong places,
And put up a false front,
Take the log out from your eye,
Before you complain about your brother's,
Cause what you do will come round,
Back to haunt you,
Nothing hidden under your bed,
Will one day be revealed,
So why don't you do good,
And purge your conscience,
So that your night's sleep,
Will be so very sweet,
And if we do not do what others may follow,
The world will be definitely a better place to live in.

THE FAMILY - A CENTRE OF INFLUENCE

In the western context, when you hit 18,
You are already considered an adult and should be treated as one,
You are expected to make your own money,
Find your own place to stay and be independent,
I am not against all that but the chinese are a different lot,
It's only when you are married are you considered independent,
At most times, you still stay with your in-laws even though you are married,
With strings attached, do you still rely on your parents for moral support?
Do you move away from your comfort zone to be really independent?
Children nowadays are a pampered lot,
They have their parents to plan everything for them,
With so much to depend on, will they grow up to be able to fend for themselves?
From young, children should not be spared the cane but learn the basics of life.
It is thru this knowledge they will develop their minds and learn to be independent.

I have been to China and noticed that their families are a very different lot,
In times of need, they will band together to resolve problems together,
In times of celebration, they will also band together to celebrate.
You can count on your friends/relations to loan that needed money in times of need,
But they will expect you to return them the favor sometime in future.
What is happening to the rest of the world?

The only way to raise funds is to talk to a banker.
"Unity in strength"
Take a chopstick and you can easily bend it.
But take a bunch of chopsticks and try to do the same?

This world is full of instant gratification,
You have instant marriages,
And instant divorces,
When things go wrong you will bail out straightaway,
But have you spare a thought for your children?
I never say mine was perfect in the first place,
But when I have children,
There is no such word as 'divorce',
No matter how difficult is the going,
Marriage is a sanctury,
With children, it is in eternity.
I never believe in breaking one's family,
"A Happy family is a "blessed" family.

WHAT IS LOVE?

It is love at first sight,
Infatuation - when your hearts beat faster,
And that rush of chemistry thru your brains,
Sent you in eternal blisshood,
A sense of longing,
The feeling of missing someone you love,
During courtship, its the mighty might,
To bring down the stars for your love one.
After marriage, and after things are settled in,
Comes the commitment, sacrifices and reality,
When love doesn't comes with the intensity,
The chemistry and the longing,
You suddenly wakeup to the wrong side of bed,
When the dust settles, do you still cling on to your marriage or move on?
Man and woman are two different creatures,
For man, it's the physical love,
And woman, the emotional love,
Two different views,
Two different requirements,
Do you see eye to eye?
Ask any couple who has spent a lifetime together,
What are their secrets,
They will tell you,
It's sacrifice, commitment, faithfulness, love and companionship.
The willingness to stay together no matter what comes may,
A Lifetime of sacrifices,
That is not what love is today.

THERE IS NO SHORTCUT TO SUCCESS

Thruout my lifetime,
I have searching for that shortcut,
You name it, I have tried it but without success,
Even with the most powerful software to visualise,
There isn't a shortcut to success.
Unless you are born with a silver spoon,
But even you have money today doesn't mean you have it tomorrow,
Unless you are prudent and know how to manage it,
For the rest of us, it's carrying our cross,
And make our living as anyone else.
The secret to success is hard work,
Day by day you build your wealth,
Solving problems by problems,
Remember you need to cross that bridge,
Before you reach the next stage,
And if you fail it will set you back,
If you are not able to climb back up,
You are already a failure,
Cause Life is a series of bridges you must cross,
And never look back,
That is the challenge of success,
With logical planning and hard work,
And a little bit of luck,
The next bridge you cross may bring you great tidings,
Or your next windfall.

You need to save enough cash of at least 6 months your salary, in order to tide over a rainy day. And after that learn all the rules in investment, buy assets not liabilities and slowly built up your cash, invest in yourself to learn a High Income skill by mentoring those who already has experience walking the pathway. Passive income is derived from sound fundamentals not speculation, by not stopping at lifelong learning, you will definitely find success in your lifetime.

THE FUTURE IS BLOCKCHAIN, AI AND MACHINE LEARNING POWERED BY AI ARCHITECTURE AND HARDWARE FOR DATACENTRES

The Andriod OS is not suited to handle multiple threads and multi-tasking well so in the future, can Harmony OS do it? The trend is for the ROM to be intergrated with RAM when the memory limitations are removed with more advanced data transmission technologies that the OS can harness. Windows 10 OS can do it but it gets more and more resource hungry and totay's SSD still has some way to go before it can better handle rapid multitasking threads. Software will always be ahead of Hardware and the Architecture to handle millions of threads under Neuromorphic computers has yet to be defined but the closest is Intel/Nvidia solution with GPU solution for Artificial Intelligence with Machine Learning which is now incorporated into Datacentres in the cloud. In the future, other playrs like IBM and Chinese chips will come in but I doubt the exposure will be great due to their limitations of softwares and applications unless there is widespread adoption by developers. Most cloud solution providers like AWS, Alibaba, Google, Microsoft at present still does not have a full suit of applications to handle AI and Machine Learning.

YOU DO NOT NEED YOUR PASSPORT ANYMORE

With advances in technology, it is possible to clear customs and checkpoints without passport anymore. The merging of all these technologies will mean there is totally no way you can beat the system, which encompasses the following;

1) A body scan to identify if you are carrying a foreign object via Xrays.
2) Facial recognition to confirm your identity.
3) Fingerprint scan to double check.
4) Voice recognition to double confirm.
5) Even if someone is smart enough in the future to fake all of the above, there is no way you can fake your DNA, not in 1000 years, and samples can be easily obtained by swaps, creating a central database of every individual on earth.

There is totally no way you can beat the system, which will be 100% accurate, there is no way you can fake everything of the above, which is linked to an advanced Artificial Intelligence system with machine learning capabilities, total 100% security with minimum manpower, it can even solve US - Mexican border problems, it is stupid to build a dumb wall costing billions when it does not get to the root of the problem. Contributed by Oogle.

PS : All these technologies are not invasive and is even better than trying to microchip you, with me around, it will never happen. No more IDs, passport, credit cards etc and your smartphone can be utilised to replace all these functions with Facial Recognition and Fingerprint sensors to approve transactions because if you lose your smartphone, nobody can utilise it. Therefore the entire ecosystem *will be changed, on how crime will be fought and there will be no escape for criminals or terrorists because there is no way to beat the system. ATMs will not exists in the future and everything will be transacted using digital currency.*

THE CITY OF THE FUTURE WILL BE RUN BY AI, MACHINE LEARNING, BLOCKCHAIN ON NEXT GEN INTERNET

Networks of the future will be Blockchain and Li-Fi that can support 6G, where spectrums will be extended to everywhere there is electricity on power grids, lamp-posts will be smart with cameras, Li-Fi, that can support wireless charging anywhere, with speeds beyond your wildest imagination, where traffic management systems control both traffic on land and air, everything including traffic lights, cameras will be linked to AI for controls, from autonomous cars, buses, trains and flying cars and taxis, homes will be built in the sea on supporting platforms, and man will travel to Mars to colonise it, all these will happen before 2050. Li-Fi has the potential to scale massively with more cells per square inch and maximising the spectrum.

CONCLUSION

There is just too much information on the future of technology to be all written on my book. If you purchased my book on my book launch in February 2020, you will be able to access my Patreon Website which is daily updated by me for FREE for 1 year and all the benefits which is listed on my website. Those who buys my eBook which will be launched before Christmas 2019 will also be given Free access for 6 months. Inside contain a lot of FREE online courses which I have trained for from the Internet so you do not need to pay more to learn from me. Soon I will launch a comprehensive course on the New Economy on Udemy.com and it will be cost effective to learn everything how to "Fish" which schools of Higher Education will not teach you.

There is nothing in thia world we will leave behind except our memories when we die, live a good life and fight a good fight, do everything what you want to do when you are young not when you are old. Nothing is impossible if you plan for it. When the time comes when everything about our brain is understood, your memories and your knowledge can be transferred like a harddisk, then we will live in the digital world forever.

THE FORGOTTON

The wails of a newborn baby fills the air,
As the nurse lift the baby by its legs,
And gave it a very tight slaps,
She wrapped the baby with a clean cloth,
And hands it to the mother creator,
I can see it in her eyes,
Gleaming with a radiant smile,
A face filled with joy,
In a heavenly bliss,
Nothing in this world can compare,
This miraculous sight,
The birth of a newborn,
The aspirations of a new found parent,
A future of hope and great tidings,
Radiate across the room.

At the hospital bed,
A frail woman lay,
A woman who is advanced in age,
Lay sick in her final moments,
Her husband at her bedside,
Clapsed her wringkled hands,
Peace I can see in her eyes,
A Life well spent and blessed,
A face of inmost tranquility,
No fear of the journey beyond,
I can see, in her eyes,
When she grasp for her last breath,
And closes her eyes forever,
Tears roll down my face,
Knowing she has crossed the boundary,
The journey to world beyond.

Our Lifes are but a memory,
How fast time really flies,
In a twinkling of an eye,
We will be halfway across our journey,
The decisions we make,
The regrets of our youth,
Nothing beats having run a good race,
The memories we leave behind,
Friends and relations we make,
Will be forever edged in their minds,
It is sad that nowadays people are so preoccupied,
With the things of the world,
They have no time left,
To feed their spiritual souls,
When the time comes,
They will become - "The Forgotten".

MY FIRST VISION

I was given a insight of,
A fighter aircraft so advanced,
That everything was controlled by,
Hundreds of applications a second,
Targeting is via,
Using the eyes on the screen,
And the controls are,
Unlike anything I have ever seen,
This aircraft is powered,
Not by the jet engine,
And it achieved speeds of,
More than 10 times the speed of sound,
The aircraft is very silent,
But I am unable to tell,
What fuel it uses,
It is able to hover,
Bank and turn,
At a tremendous speed,
But it is not shaped,
Like a UFO.

MY SECOND VISION

I was very disturbed,
By my second vision,
And I get paranoid,
When someone else,
Is able to tell what I had seen,
It's about Mind Control,
The manipulation of your senses,
The insertion of thoughts,
The hearing of voices,
Telling you to do the things you do,
Until you cannot tell what is real or not,
The introduction of virtual,
Can be abused,
Let's guard against,
The corners of our mind.
Never believe what you hear or see,
Cause "signs and wonders",
Can also be manipulated,
Deceiving the elected too.

MY THIRD VISION

In the age to come,
Man will be lord over space and time,
After the transformation,
In a shield of Light,
Travel will be but in a twightling of an eye.
He who has the wisdom,
In the coming of age,
The Angel of Light will also teach his people,
About aliens and UFO,
Travel between space and time,
Going into another dimension,
Denying the existence of God,
Hereby robbing you,
A higher ground,
Your rightful place in the universe.
All powers and principalities,
Are placed by God,
The training of the elect,
For a camel to enter,
The eye of a needle.

MY FOURTH VISION

Is concerning myself,
The journeys I got to make,
My higher calling,
How every member of my family,
Will turn their back on me,
I have given up everything,
Very disappointed with my family,
The cares of the material world,
How shortsighted can they be,
It is but spiritual warfare,
And a mask has covered their eyes,
If given a lifeline I can turn,
The collapse of my business,
A mountain of debts,
That is artificially influenced,
Until I don't have a single penny,
Even don't have food to eat,
They think they can control me,
Each pushing their own agenda,
By restricting me access to money,
I will be forced to remain in Singapore.
You can use money to create lies,
But I am even greater than the elite,
Cause I know all the Truth.
I will leave my family,
And will do the most drastic,
I will turn my backs on them,
Becoming a citizen of another,
To another place far away,
Providing solutions to the world,
Solving the world's problems,
Only then will everything be resolved,

MY FIFTH VISION

And God showed me a 3D Matrix,
In it contained,
All the information in the world,
You can specify in the Matrix,
Many ways to display the info,
But it will always be in a cube.
It supports multitasking,
Many screens can be opened,
The greatest data mining tool,
A search engine so advanced,
Data can be displayed,
Even links and associations,
In hundred of layers deep,
What is needed can be put aside,
The useless will be discarded,
To find every solution and answers,
Closest to the Truth.

www.ingramcontent.com/pod-product-compliance
Lightning Source LLC
Chambersburg PA
CBHW030840180526
45163CB00004B/1403